Teaching Mathematics
Through Children's Art

Doug Williams

Heinemann
Portsmouth, NH

Heinemann
A division of Reed Elsevier Inc.
361 Hanover Street
Portsmouth, NH 03801-3912

Offices and agents throughout the world

Published simultaneously in the
United States in 1995
by Heinemann
and in Australia by
Oxford University Press
253 Normanby Road
South Melbourne
Victoria, Australia 3205

First published in 1990 by
Oxford University Press

Typeset by Solo Typesetting, South Australia
Printed by Impact Printing Victoria Pty Ltd

Library of Congress Cataloging-in-Publication Data:

Williams, Doug, 1948-
    Teaching mathematics through children's art / Doug
Williams.
        p.   cm.
    Originally published: South Melbourne, Vic., Australia:
Oxford University Press, 1990.
    Includes bibliographical references.
    ISBN 0-435-08368-6
    1. Art in mathematics education. 2. Mathematics - Study
and teaching (Elementary). I. Title
    QA19.A78W55 1994
372.7'044 - dc20   94-36399
                                                    CIP

•CONTENTS•

◆ ACKNOWLEDGEMENTS ◆

Some years ago when I was learning to be an art teacher, I was strongly influenced by the love and enthusiasm of Kate Hart. She showed me the starting points for good art teaching and her influences permeate this book.

In the same way this book is a starting point for good classroom teachers. Good teachers will want to make these units their own by adding and subtracting to complement their own style and interests. This process was begun in the developmental stages of this book by Lynette Wade, Pembroke Primary School, whose resounding support encouraged me greatly and who has been directly responsible for the two 'Picasso' lessons in the unit *Twists and Turns*, and for several photographs in the book.

My thanks go to these two friends; to Sue Gibson; to several other colleagues who reviewed the draft material; and to my favourite typist, Jean Lardner.

Doug Williams

◆ INTRODUCTION ◆

In my teaching career I have spent many years specialising in mathematics teaching, many other years specialising in art/craft teaching and still more years as a classroom teacher. This book attempts to draw together all those experiences to provide a framework of activities which will enrich, but not supplant, any teacher's classroom.

At the back of my mind in the preparation of this material were three generalisations, which I present for your consideration:

◆ most children enjoy art activities
◆ too many children learn to dislike mathematics
◆ teachers enjoy working across curriculum areas when they feel that good teaching is proceeding in each area.

I also work from a philosophy which I would like to share with you. It has two simple parts:

◆ the teacher is the pinnacle of the education process
◆ good teaching comes before good learning.

The differences between good art teaching and good mathematics teaching are not as great as you may have thought. Both are based on the following:

◆ Shared language (teacher ↔ child, child ↔ child) is the foundation of learning.
◆ Problem-solving is used to stimulate and challenge.
◆ Planned experiences with many materials are provided to
  (i) develop concepts
  (ii) practise skills.

There are some differences though in the concepts and skills developed in each discipline.

Art concepts	*Art skills*
line	awareness
shape	change
colour	contrast
pattern	decoration
texture	quality
	special effects

Each skill can be applied to each concept and represents something of a gradation in the maturity of learning. For example:

- children must first become **aware** of **line**
- then they can learn to **change lines** or change things with lines
- a developing language concerning **contrasting lines** (curved/straight, long/short, spiky/bumpy) leads to experimenting using **lines** for appropriate **decoration**
- experimenting with decoration leads to judgements about whether the **lines** used are right for the piece of work—a **quality** judgement
- and a developing understanding of quality leads to controlled use of **lines** to obtain desired or **special effects**.

What makes teaching exciting is that all these experiences are actually non-linear.

Maths concepts	*Maths skills*
collections (sets)	sorting/classifying
relations	counting
number	operations
pattern	measuring
space	symbolizing
time	representing

With mathematics too there is something of a hierarchy implied, but again nothing which suggests that teaching should be lock-step linear. The human mind makes leaps of faith and connections between apparently isolated pieces of information on a daily basis. That is what makes living exciting!

Making use of this book

Let me make it quite clear from the beginning that I am not suggesting that all mathematics could or should be taught in or through relationships with art or vice versa. The source of each set of lessons is either good mathematics or good art. The result of each set followed through in the classroom, is good learning in both subject areas; and usually a theme which is a rich source of activities in language and other disciplines.

Steps:

1 Choose a partner or team. You can successfully use these activities by yourself, but you will benefit much more by working co-operatively with colleagues.

2 Choose a unit suitable for the level you teach. Read it through with your colleagues; discuss the suggestions critically; brainstorm and list any associated ideas which you have.

3 Plan a sequence of lessons across curriculum areas. Use the steps as a guide; alter as you see fit; add your own ideas.

4 Execute the plan and continue meeting to appraise and replan as you gauge the children's learning.

When do you stop?

Some activities will lead to themes which maintain children's interest for a very long time. Others may last only two or three lessons. There is no need to continue to try to teach something through an activity which is waning. There are many ways of teaching anything. Rest from the particular concept or skill, and try a different method some time in the future.

◆ SCOPE AND SEQUENCE CHART ◆

Year Level	Unit Title	Mathematics Content	Art/Craft Content
Beginners/1	Stringing It Out	◆ Problem-solving (2D) ◆ Inventing patterns ◆ Measurement (informal units) ◆ Relations (e.g. 'is bigger than')	◆ Awareness of line and shape ◆ Changing line ◆ Decoration of line ◆ Decoration with pattern
Beginners/1	Pastel Creatures	◆ Sorting and classifying ◆ Ordering and ordinal number ◆ One-to-one and many-to-one correspondence ◆ Problem-solving ◆ Counting and simple operations ◆ Visual representation	◆ Awareness of texture ◆ Decoration with line, colour and pattern ◆ Changing shape
1/2	Colourful Numbers	◆ Counting ◆ Number sentences	◆ Changing shape ◆ Decoration with line, colour, shape and pattern
2/3	Whose Feet Are These?	◆ Counting in groups (twos, fives, tens) ◆ Measuring heights (formally in centimetres or informally with other standards) ◆ Visual representation	◆ Decoration with line, colour and pattern
3–6	Modellene Markers	◆ Review of number facts ◆ Measurement in centimetres	◆ Changing shape in 3D ◆ Decoration with shape, colour and pattern
3/4	Knot A Problem	◆ Length measurement using formal units smaller and larger than one metre ◆ Visual representation	◆ Changing lines ◆ Contrasting lines ◆ Decoration with lines

Year Level	Unit Title	Mathematics Content	Art/Craft Content
3/4	Twists And Turns	◆ Exploring reflection (symmetry) ◆ Exploring rotation (pattern) ◆ Measurement in centimetres ◆ Number facts	◆ Decoration with line, colour and shape ◆ Contrasting lines and shapes
5/6	Circulation	◆ Number facts ◆ Visual representation ◆ Mathematics of the circle ◆ Problem-solving	◆ Changing circles ◆ Decoration with line, shape, colour and pattern ◆ Contrasting shape and colour
5/6	Something Fishy About Fractions * This unit emphasises the *Co-operative Group Learning* teaching strategy	◆ Fraction language as part of a whole ◆ Equivalence of fractions ◆ Addition and subtraction of fractions	◆ Changing shape ◆ Decoration with pattern and colour ◆ Quality of decoration
5/6	Milk Carton Mathematics	◆ 3D geometric language ◆ Problem-solving ◆ Pattern investigations	◆ Changing shape in 3D ◆ Decoration with line and pattern
5/6	Number Machines	◆ Number facts ◆ Pattern investigations ◆ Problem-solving	◆ Special effects with line ◆ Decoration with line, shape and colour

GLOSSARY

◆ Paper

bulky news   a cheaper quality drawing paper.

cartridge paper   a more expensive, heavier-weight and whiter drawing paper.

cover paper   similar to cartridge paper, in a variety of colours. Often used for construction and collage.

kindergarten squares   light-weight paper squares, coloured on one side. Used for decoration and collage.

◆ Adhesives

PVA glue   white Poly Vinyl Adhesive. Used in woodwork, suitable for collage.

clag   paste used to adhere paper to paper. Often home-made with flour and water.

Blu-tack   reusable rubbery substance used to attach posters, etc. to all sorts of surfaces without leaving marks.

sticky tape   clear adhesive tape on a roll.

◆ Others

lengths of wool   any yarn or string can be used.

netball court   about the same size as a basketball court, divided into thirds.

worm measuring   see illustration, page 11.

display board   any classroom board or wall reserved for displaying children's work.

Modellene   modelling compound which is a cross between plasticine and clay. Malleable at room temperature and becomes hard when baked. Available in many colours, often used for making small models and jewellery.

Modellene markers   small models made from Modellene and used to mark a player's place on a game board.

trundle wheel   wheel with a 1-metre circumference with a handle attached. As it is rolled it clicks every time 1 metre is travelled.

HB pencils   a 'grey lead' pencil (HB indicates grade of colour and hardness of lead).

drawing pins   short flat-headed pins used to attach posters, etc. to display boards.

dead matches   used matches.

Snap   a card game: Deal shuffled cards equally amongst players. Players gather their packs but do not look at their cards. At a rapid pace players take turns to place their top card face-up in the centre. Continue until a pair of cards (e.g. two tens) follow each other. The first person to slap their hand on the centre pile and calls 'Snap!' wins all those cards and adds them to the bottom of their pack. This person continues the game by placing his/her top card in the centre, with other players following. The game continues until one player has won all the cards.
   (A player who runs out of cards is out of the game.)

Concentration   a card game: Place each card face-down in a rectangular array. Players take turns to select two cards and turn them over. If cards are a pair (e.g. two tens), player may keep them and select another two cards. If cards don't match they are turned face-down again and next player has a turn. The idea is to concentrate on the location of cards as they are turned over to try to make a match when it is your turn. The game continues until all cards are chosen. The winner is the person with the most pairs.

1

◆ STRINGING IT OUT ◆

Year Level:	Beginners or Year 1
Minimum Number of Lessons:	5
Art Concepts/Skills:	◆ Awareness of line and shape
	◆ Changing line
	◆ Decoration of line
	◆ Decoration with pattern
Maths Concepts/Skills:	◆ Problem-solving (2D)
	◆ Inventing patterns
	◆ Measurement (informal units)
	◆ Relations (e.g. 'is bigger than')

◆ LESSON 1 ◆

Concepts/Skills	◆ Awareness of line, shape
	◆ Changing line
	◆ Problem-solving in 2D space
Equipment	Bulky News paper about 28 cm x 38 cm, lengths of wool about 40 cm (make them colourful), Cel-mix or wallpaper paste (one container per table), table cleaning cloths, art smocks.

Activity

1   *Take a string and place it on your paper so that it is straight. Can you make it straight in another direction? How about a third way? How many ways do you think the string could be placed on the paper so it was straight?*
    Discuss.

2   *Now make your string*
    ◆ *wavy*
    ◆ *pointed*
    ◆ *hilly*
    ◆ *cloudy*
    ◆ *spiralled*
    ◆ *something different.*

3   *Use your string to make the paper have **two** parts. Can you do this another way? Can you do it with a curved (straight) string?*

4   *Can you use the string to make the paper have **three** parts?*

5   *Now you can use two strings. Can you make*
    ◆ *four parts*
    ◆ *three parts*
    ◆ *five parts?*

6   *Use any number of strings to make*
    ◆ *eight parts*
    ◆ *seven parts.*

7   To complete this lesson, show the children how to push their strings into the Cel-mix and arrange them as different types of lines on their Bulky News (five strings are enough). The strings may be lightly tapped with a finger to help them stick. These pictures will take about three days to dry. The teacher needs a picture too.

8   Throughout this activity the teacher should move among the children; compliment and encourage; draw attention to the **variety** of solutions; encourage the children once or twice to move around and learn from one another.

◆ LESSON 2 ◆

Concepts/Skills
- ◆ Measurement (informal units)
- ◆ Relations ('is shorter than')

Equipment
Balls of wool, scissors, Bulky News (or computer paper), small staplers, writing- and/or drawing-tools.

Activity

1 *Cut a piece of wool which is about as long as your paper.*

2 *Walk around the room (outside, up the hall etc.) and find something longer than your string. Come back and tell me what you've found.*

  The teacher should observe the children's comparison methods. Emphasise stretching the string so it is taut.

  Now find me something shorter than your string.

3 *I want each of you to measure three things which are shorter than your string. Remember what they are, then come back to your place.*

  The teacher should ask some children to tell about their three things.

4 To complete this activity, demonstrate to the children how to safely staple their string to their paper. Then on the paper they write about, or draw, the three things shorter than their string.

◆ LESSON 3 ◆

Concepts/Skills
- ◆ Measurement (informal units)
- ◆ Relations ('is longer than')

Equipment
Balls of wool, scissors, strips of paper on which a sentence can be written, writing-tools, staplers. The children will need a partner.

Activity

1 *Cut a piece of wool that is so long that it takes two of you to make it straight.*

2 *Now find some things that your string is longer than. Is it longer than*
  ◆ *the table*
  ◆ *the chalkboard*
  ◆ *the room*
  ◆ *the netball court?*

3 Back at the table the children fold their sentence-paper in half lengthwise. Depending on the children's abilities, the teacher may have already done this.
  On one side write your names.
  On the other side write a sentence which tells one thing your string is longer than, e.g. This string is longer than the board.
  Again, depending on the children's abilities, the teacher may have prepared part of the sentence or may have parents in to help.

4 *Now hang your sentence-paper over the string and add a staple at each end so it won't fall off, but will slide on the string.*

5 Display the children's strings.

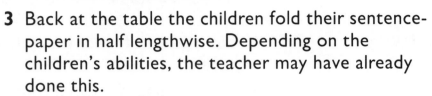

staple

◆ LESSON 4 ◆

Concepts/Skills ◆ Measurement (informal units)

Equipment Balls of wool, scissors, writing-paper, writing-tools, line-markings such as a netball court.

Discussion The teacher cuts a piece of wool which can be stretched straight.

I am going to count how many of these strings fit along this line.

The teacher should deliberately make mistakes, such as leaving large gaps between the start of one measuring unit and the end of the previous one. Encourage the children to tell you how to carefully measure and count.

Demonstrate 'worm' measuring.

Activity	**1** The children each cut a piece of wool which they can stretch straight.
	2 They measure and count how many times their string fits into various lines.
	3 The teacher chooses one line and each child counts how many times their string fits along this line, and then writes a sentence about it.

◆ LESSON 5 ◆

Concepts/Skills
- ◆ Decoration of line
- ◆ Decoration with pattern
- ◆ Inventing patterns

Equipment
String picture made in Lesson 1, markers, demonstration paper and easel (or board and chalk) for the teacher.

Discussion
The teacher uses the paper and easel to ask questions like:
I'm going to make this mark here. ⬭ *Who could do another one next to it? Could someone do another one? What might come next? Who could repeat this?*

What about this?

Do you know what we have been doing here?

Emphasise the idea of making patterns by doing something again and again—a pattern repeats.

The teacher now demonstrates how to add patterns to the strings using the markers, e.g.

The teacher need not complete this, but should emphasise variety of colour and mark to let the pattern grow.

Activity

The children complete their own string picture patterns.

Add name tags to the children's work and display them.

Karen, Beginners

◆ EXTENSIONS ◆

- ◆ Hanging objects on a line (ordinal number), e.g. washing.
- ◆ Giving children a pastel line on a piece of drawing-paper and asking them to turn it into a picture of something with pastels.

- ◆ Stories, e.g. Marion Holland, *A Big Ball of String, A Beginner Book*, Random House 1958.
- ◆ Games involving lines.
- ◆ Animals which make lines, e.g. snail trails, paw prints.
- ◆ Lining up machines, e.g. train and carriages, parking cars.

2

◆ PASTEL CREATURES ◆

Year Level:	Beginners or Year 1
Minimum Number of Lessons:	5
Art Concepts/Skills:	◆ Awareness of texture ◆ Decoration with line, colour and pattern ◆ Changing shape
Maths Concepts/Skills:	◆ Sorting and classifying ◆ Ordering and ordinal number ◆ One-to-one and many-to-one correspondence ◆ Problem-solving ◆ Counting and simple operations ◆ Visual representation

◆ LESSON 1 ◆

Concepts/Skills ◆ Awareness of shape and texture

Equipment One newspaper per child (referred to as a newspaper-pad), cheap drawing-paper (computer paper with edges sliced off in a trimmer is a good source), cover paper (or similar) for a chart, paste, scissors, thick oil-pastels (minimum of one box per four children), soap and towels.

Activity

1 Unless they are taught the potential of the medium, children will automatically use the end of the pastel (as they use a pencil) and consequently produce infantile line-drawings. The colour is the full length of the pastel piece (unlike a pencil where it is only at the end), so children have to be taught to use the pastel on its **side**.

To prepare for drawing, the new pastel should be broken in two and have all the paper removed. Also, to make more intense marks, the children should draw with their drawing-paper on top of a newspaper-pad.

2 The following sequence, when repeated over two or three lessons, will produce some remarkable artwork:

(a) Demonstrate a mark made with the side of a pastel.
How did my hand move? Show me in the air. Now see if you can make a mark like this on your paper.

(b) *Make up your own mark. Now show it to the person next to you and tell them how you did it. See if they can copy yours. You try to do theirs.*

(c) *Make up lots more marks of your own.*
It is very important to compliment and encourage every effort at this stage.

(d) *Can you do*
◆ *a fluffy mark*   ◆ *a spiky mark*
◆ *a twisting mark*   ◆ *a wavy mark?*
◆ *a curly mark*
Encourage the children to learn from each other.

(e) Make a chart of interesting marks that the children create. They could either cut around their marks and paste them on the chart, or redraw them directly on the chart. Remind them to use the side of the pastel. Add some more marks of your own if necessary to widen the children's views.

(f) Discuss names which could be given to each mark. Try to use adjectives.

(g) Study the chart.
How was this mark made? Show me in the air. Now try to draw it yourself. You may use any colour.

(h) *Look at it this way ↑ , this way →, this way ↓ , and this way ← until it makes you think of something. Finish the drawing to show me what it is.*

Teachers can encourage more expansive and detailed drawings when the children say they've finished, by asking questions like:
Can you show me where it lives?
What other things might be there?
What sort of clothes are your people wearing?
Can you draw the rest of the family for me?
The children may add smaller detail with the end of the pastel.

Brian, Beginners

◆ LESSON 2 ◆

Concepts/Skills
◆ Awareness of texture
◆ Decoration with pattern, colour and line
◆ Changing shape

Equipment
Newspaper-pads, cartridge about 28 cm x 38 cm, oil-pastels (thick), food dye in various colours at a 'station' protected by newspaper or plastic, brushes or sponges.

Activity

1 After at least three lessons turning pastel marks into pictures, the children will be ready to make some excellent creatures to be used for mathematics. The sequence for creating the creatures could go like this:

(a) *Choose your favourite mark from the chart and draw it on your paper.*
Alternatively the teacher could randomly supply each child with a predrawn mark.

(b) Select one child's mark and gather the children around.
Jenny's mark is the start of some sort of creature. Let's look at it in different ways until you know what animal it is and what part she has drawn. Put up your hand when you see something.

(c) Ask one child to explain what they see and encourage detail.
Where will the head be? How many legs will you see? What type of skin does it have— lumpy, scaly, hairy, slimy? What is the creature doing?
Repeat this type of discussion with starting points drawn by at least two other children.

(d) *Now go back to your table and show me how your mark can be turned into a creature.*

It might be
- *a farm animal*
- *a bush animal*
- *an undersea creature*
- *a pet animal*
- *an insect*
- *a flying creature.*

(e) *Don't forget*
- *eyes*
- *ears*
- *horns*
- *skin*
- *claws*
- *wings*

You may use the end of the pastel to add some of these details. But you don't have to show me where it lives.

2 To finish off the creatures, the paper can be brushed or sponged with food dye. (It will help the mathematics lessons if there are a variety of colours from which each child chooses one.) The oil-pastel resists the dye and the dye creates a vivid background which greatly increases the children's satisfaction with their art.

An eating monster
David, Beginners

◆ LESSON 3 ◆

Concepts/Skills
- ◆ Sorting and classifying
- ◆ Counting
- ◆ Visual representation

Equipment   Pastel creatures, pins, display-board.

Activity

1 There are several lessons involved in this activity, since each day a different attribute can be used as the basis of the sort.

   These lessons are designed with a small group in mind.

2 Ask the children to sort the creatures into those which belong together. What are **their** categories? Discuss alternatives such as
   - ◆ type (bush, farm etc.)
   - ◆ colour
   - ◆ background colour
   - ◆ shape
   - ◆ type of skin
   - ◆ skin pattern (spots, stripes etc.)
   - ◆ number of legs
   - ◆ side view/front view
   - ◆ size.

3 Once sorted, each set could be sorted again. For example if the first sort was on the basis of background colour, then within each colour group the creatures could be organised into skin type— the smooth skins here; the hairies there; this pile for the spiky ones.

4 Whichever level of sorting is used, the members of each subset of the sort could be counted and recorded.

   Discuss which group has more or less.

5 Once the creatures have been sorted, it is very easy to pin them to a display board to make a vertical or horizontal 'graph of the day'. The next

time the creatures are sorted, the labelling will be different and the graph can be oriented differently, i.e. if it is horizontal today it can be vertical the next time.

◆ LESSON 4 ◆

Concepts/Skills	◆ Sorting and classifying ◆ Simple operations
Equipment	Pastel creatures, something to use as a fence (e.g. a ruler).
Activity	1 As with the previous lesson, this type of activity should be repeated frequently.

2 Sort the creatures.

3 *Count the number of creatures in this set. This one is tired and has gone home to bed* (take it away). *Guess the number of creatures still here.*
Discuss with the children the strategies they used to make the guess.
How could we check your guess?
Allow the children to count again.

4 Another type of activity which can be used once the creatures have been sorted, is a model of addition.
Today there is a fence between these two groups of creatures. Count the creatures on this side of the fence. Now count the creatures on that side of the fence.
I am going to take the fence away so that the creatures can play together. Guess the number of creatures altogether.
Discuss with the children the strategies they used to make the guess.
How could we check your guess?
Allow the children to count again.

◆ LESSON 5 ◆

Concepts/Skills
- ◆ Ordering and ordinal number
- ◆ One-to-one and many-to-one correspondence
- ◆ Problem-solving

Equipment   Pastel creatures, counters in two colours.

Activity

1 Place the creatures in a line (unsorted) and decide which end is the start. Try ordering activities like:
   - ◆ *touch the fourth creature*
   - ◆ *turn the third one over*
   - ◆ *hide the first creature behind this bush* (provide a small branch).

2 This can be combined with a language activity if you make up a story about the animals all going somewhere (e.g. the Grand Final of the football) and then include things which happen to them. For example the sixth animal decides to catch a train rather than walk (turn it over).

   The children soon get the idea and can help invent the story and carry out the mathematics.

*A hairy monster
David, Beginners*

3 A different type of activity, which involves correspondence, can also be carried out with the creatures. They don't have to be in a line for this. *Today our creatures have to be fed. These red counters are their pretend food. Each creature must have one piece of food. Mary, would you like to feed the creatures?*

4 *They need a drink too. These blue counters are a pretend bowl of water. They are allowed one bowl each. Alphonso, would you like to give the creatures their drink?*

5 Many-to-one correspondence can also be experienced if the creatures are allowed more than one piece of food, or more than one type of food (e.g. red counters and green counters).

6 Problem-solving is involved with questions like: *We have all this food for the creatures today* (a container of red counters). *They all have to get the same amount of food or else they fight. How can we share the food?*
Discuss the children's strategies.

◆ EXTENSIONS ◆

- ◆ Keep classroom pets.
- ◆ Organise a pet day.
- ◆ Visit the Zoo or an animal sanctuary.
- ◆ Write sentences about each child's creature.
- ◆ Read animal stories.
- ◆ Make up animal dances.
- ◆ Bend and stretch like animals.
- ◆ Have animal races (e.g. crab, kangaroo, horse).
- ◆ Make animals with paper or other material which can be changed to make different skins.

3

◆ COLOURFUL NUMBERS ◆

Year Level:	Year 1 or 2
Minimum Number of Lessons:	6
Art Concepts/Skills:	◆ Changing shape
	◆ Decoration with line, colour, shape and pattern
Maths Concepts/Skills:	◆ Counting
	◆ Number sentences

◆ LESSONS 1 and 2 ◆

Concepts/Skills
◆ Changing shape
◆ Decoration with line, colour, shape and pattern

Equipment
Newspaper-pads (see Lesson 1, *Pastel Creatures*), oil-pastels and/or markers and/or pencils and/or crayons, coloured paper, 'junk' items for collage, material scraps, scissors, PVA glue, clag, cartridge paper and cover paper about 28 cm x 38 cm, precut circles if available.

Activity
1 *Today you are going to choose one thing to draw or make. You are going to draw or make it with as much detail as you can and then you are going to repeat it on your page until the page is full, or your time runs out.*

You might do an animal, a car, a flower, a face, a plane, a shoe, or anything else. Look at all this equipment here and tell me what ideas you have.

2 Discuss the suggestions made by three or four children. Be sure to encourage detail in their object and explanation of the materials they think they might use.

3 The children make their number picture. The teacher assists by encouraging detail and helping to solve problems.

4 Lesson 2 is a repeat of Lesson 1 (with less need for introduction).

When both lessons are complete, each child should have two pictures, each one illustrating a different object repeated a number of times.

Number pictures by Year 2 children (from Ann & Johnny Baker, Young Australia Maths, Level Two, Thomas Nelson Australia)

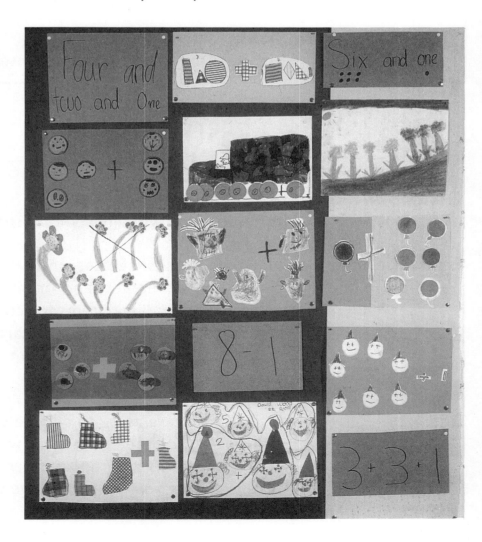

◆ LESSONS 3 to 6 ◆

Concepts/Skills
- ◆ Creating number sentences
- ◆ Counting

Equipment

Number pictures, numeral cards 1 – 10 (for a class of thirty children you will need six sets), rectangles of card or paper about 20 cm x 5 cm, markers or crayons, wool or string, strips of paper about 1 cm wide, Blu-tack.

Note: Blu-tack is used because whatever the children do to their number picture has to be non-permanent so that it can be used again. This lesson can be used many times and achieve a different result each time. However, if teachers wish to use it only once, then the wool, strips of paper and Blu-tack are unnecessary.

Activity

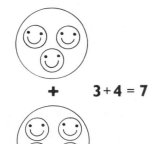

+   **3 + 4 = 7**

1 *Can anyone tell me a number story which equals 7 (or any other number)?*

Accept and illustrate some suggestions with sketches, e.g.

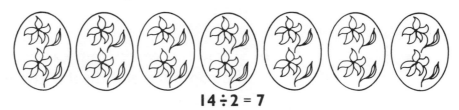

14 ÷ 2 = 7

2 If possible, the teacher should have some drawings prepared which equal the chosen number. Hold each one up and ask:

What number story about 7 do these represent? e.g.

3 Select one of the children's number pictures and ask that child to select a numeral card from the pack.

Now we have to try to find a number story which equals this number (the chosen card) *in your picture. Can you help me do it?*

With the help of this child, and the rest of the class, work out a number story and display it by sectioning with wool or crossing out with paper strips if necessary. Write the number story on the rectangle of paper and Blu-tack it to the bottom of the picture.

Note: If it is not possible with reasonable effort to create a number story for the chosen card, then it is replaced and a new card is drawn.

4 Repeat step **3** with another picture and another child.

5 Organise the children into pairs. Issue them with both their number pictures and allow them to choose two numeral cards each. They now work out, record, and attach a number story to each picture.

6 Staple the work from each pair back to back along the top edge and display them from a string across the room.

7 As part of each maths lesson for the following few days, take down some of the pictures and ask the pairs involved to talk about their number sentence and how they created it.

8 When these sentences have been thoroughly explored, the pictures can be taken down and stripped of their wool and paper strips.

Then they can be re-issued with new numeral cards, and new pairs can repeat the whole activity.

◆ EXTENSIONS ◆

◆ Issue children with a card which says '2 frogs', '5 cars', '3 clowns' etc. Ask them to write a story about their card which uses as many numbers as possible, e.g.

'Once upon a time a racing driver had **five** cars. He crashed **one** at Sandown, so he only had **four**. But his sponsor gave him **two** more practise cars, so then he had **six** . . .'

◆ While the children's pictures are on display, record their number sentences on the same size cards as the numeral cards. Then arrange packs of sentences with corresponding answer cards so that the children can play Snap or Concentration in small groups.

◆ 'Find the Sign' and 'Number of the Day' from Doug Williams, *Cal.Q.Lator, Your Classroom Companion*, Oxford University Press 1987, pp. 23′–4, reproduced below.

Find the Sign

Aim

Once the meanings of the four operations have been understood, to practise their use within the number range set down.

Activity

The teacher prepares cards showing what has been pressed and what is displayed, such as:

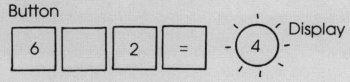

But the card does not show which operation button has been pressed. The children use their calculator and trial and error to find the missing sign.

Variation

1. This can be made into a game between two children. Player A uses the calculator to make up and secretly record an equation. Player A then shows player B the recorded equation without the operation sign. Player B uses the calculator to rediscover the equation. One point is given for each attempt. A points tally is kept and the player with the lowest score wins.

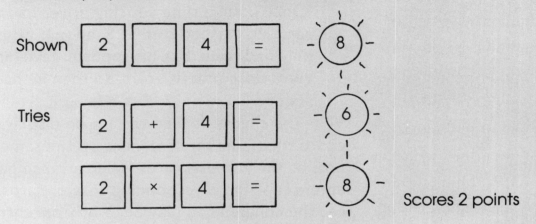

Shown

Tries

Scores 2 points

2. Use the same idea for a missing number in an equation, such as:

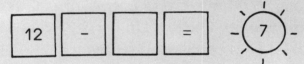

Number of the Day

Aim

To investigate numbers in the counting range.

Activity

The teacher writes a number on the board, e.g. 10. The children record all the ways they can find to make the calculator display this number, e.g. 6 + 4 = 10, 20 ÷ 2 = 10. *Be careful* to use brackets when recording children's answers. For example 2 + 3 × 2 gives an answer of 10 on the calculator because the machine reads (2 + 3) × 2. If you write just 2 + 3 × 2 when recording the child's answer the *hierarchy rule* (see page 11) *must* be applied and gives the answer 8.

4

◆ WHOSE FEET ◆
ARE THESE?

Year Level:	Year 2 or 3
Minimum Number of Lessons:	9
Art Concepts/Skills:	◆ Decoration with line, colour and pattern
Maths Concepts/Skills:	◆ Counting in groups (twos, fives and tens)
	◆ Measuring heights (formally in centimetres or informally with appropriate Cuisenaire rod or other standard)
	◆ Visual representation

◆ LESSON 1 ◆

Concepts/Skills
◆ Decoration with line, colour, pattern
◆ Measuring heights

Equipment
Reproducible Feet Sheet (see p. 31), computer paper (or other long paper), masking-tape, markers, tape-measures (or other informal standard), long strips of paper (or ribbon) for graphing. (Paper strips can easily be made by running joined computer paper through a trimmer.)

Discussion

Provide each child with a copy of the reproducible Feet Sheet and lead a discussion based on the question: *Whose feet are these?* Make a chalkboard list of reasons for having bare feet (consider other cultures too), and the characters who might belong to them. Some examples are:

◆ a pirate
◆ Mummy getting into a shower
◆ an Aborigine
◆ a surfer
◆ a baby learning to walk
◆ a person entering a Japanese temple.

Activity

1 Ask the children to choose one of the characters and tape their Feet Sheet onto the bottom of a length of computer paper. Then they draw in their character, dressing it appropriately and taping on extra sheets of computer paper if necessary.

The children should be encouraged to use as much detail and patterning as possible **but** markers should not be used for colouring in areas larger than a thumbnail.

Note: If drawing is difficult for the children, they could lie down on the computer paper and ask a friend to draw their outline. Collage could also be used to decorate the bodies.

2 Ask the children to name the character they have made. The name should try to reflect the person.

3 The children then use paper strips to measure the person from toe to head. (This is only appropriate of course if their person is standing up. If their character is sitting on a rock fishing or 'bent' in some other way, they will have to help a friend.) The character's name should be written on the paper strip and the strips saved by the teacher.

Whose Feet are These?

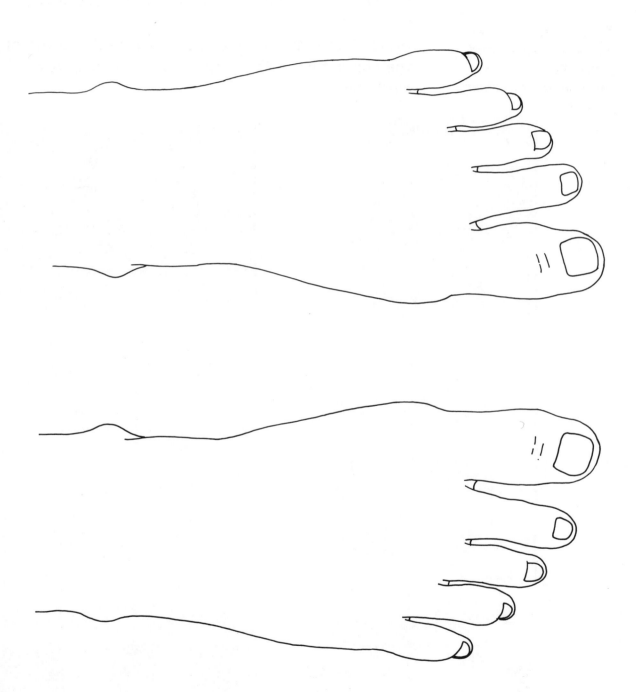

*To be enlarged on photocopier before distribution.

4 Finally the children first guess and then measure the character's height in centimetres (or other chosen standard). Both answers should be written in their workbook.

5 To complete the activity the teacher should display the characters side by side with their feet at the same level.
Note: There may only be room to display some of the characters in this way. If so, what follows can easily be adapted.

These examples were made by Lauren and Jodie, Year 1, with some help from their parents

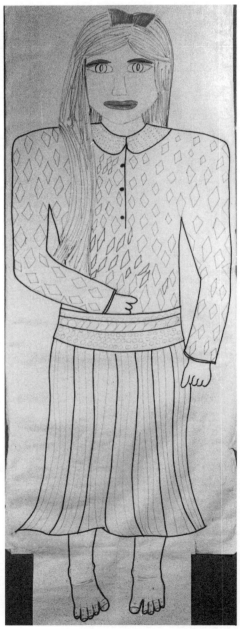
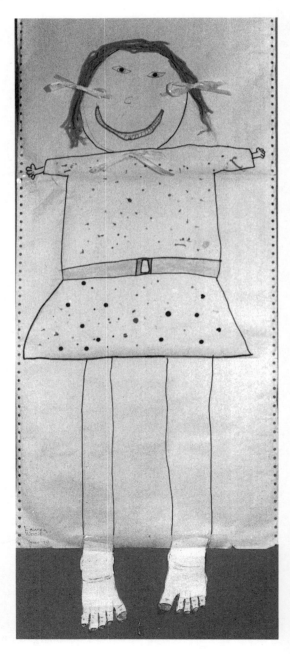

◆ LESSON 2 ◆

Concepts/Skills   ◆ Measuring heights

Equipment   Metre-rulers or tape-measures, chalk, an outside wall-space against which the children can put their backs. The children may need a partner.

Discussion   *You know your character's height in centimetres because we measured it yesterday. How tall do you think you are? Write down your guess.*
Discuss methods children might use to discover their own height.

Activity

1 The children check their guess by measuring their own height. The result is recorded.

2 Discuss with the class how their height compares with their characters.
Reginald, your character is a baby.
Does it make sense that you are shorter than a baby? How can we explain some of these surprises?
Encourage imaginative explanations such as a close-up (or long-distance) drawing; the character is a giant (or a dwarf).

3 The children write a story about themselves and their character which has to include the two height measurements.

◆ LESSON 3 ◆

Concepts/Skills   ◆ Measuring heights
◆ Visual representation

Equipment   Character strips from Lesson 1 which have been made into a bar graph by the teacher, extra paper strips, chalk, wall-space. The children may need a partner.

Discussion

These strips are a picture of the heights of your characters. Why do I have one end all in the same line?

What sort of information does the chart tells us? How can we check the information?

Do comparisons between our characters really make sense? Would it make more sense to compare each other? Why?

How can we make a paper strip to represent ourselves?

Activity

1 The children make a paper strip to represent their own height. Name it.

2 The teacher makes the strips into a graph, taking special care to review the reason for placing the bottom of all the strips at the same level.

3 Each child makes up five questions about the information in the graph. These are exchanged with their partner and answered.

◆ LESSONS 4 to 9 ◆

Concepts/Skills ◆ Counting in groups (multiplication and division)

Equipment

Display of characters made in Lesson 1, sticky tape, cards which fit neatly beneath the feet of the pictures and show:

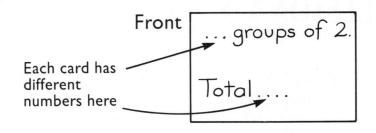

Discussion

If we wanted to count the number of feet in our character display, how would we do it?

Discuss counting by twos (and ones). Also agree on a place to start the count to be sure that none are missed.

Activity

1 Ask each child to work out which group of two their character forms within the count; find the correct card and stick it on with the 'groups of' side showing.

2 The character display is now a maths resource which can be used in many ways. For example:
   ◆ choral counting forwards and backwards from various starts;
   ◆ asking the children to write their own questions to exchange with a friend. Their questions might be:
      Which person is 7 groups of 2?
      How many groups of 2 up to the pirate?
      How many groups of 2 from the baby to the Aborigine?
      What is 3 groups of 2 plus 5 groups of 2?
   ◆ Cover the totals and play 'Tell me the Totals'. The winner is the first to answer correctly when a 'groups of 2' question is asked.
      Alternatively, cover the 'groups of' and play 'Tell me the Groups of 2'.

3 Activities such as those in step **2** should continue for many days.
   When the children's language and understanding have developed sufficiently through these **and other activities**, the cards can be turned over and used in a similar way to develop the 2-times table.

4 As the year develops the cards can also be replaced by 'groups of 5' and 'groups of 10' cards by first discussing how to count toes.

◆ EXTENSIONS ◆

- ◆ Classification of characters by features.
- ◆ Modelling characters from clay or modelling dough (e.g. Modellene or Fimo).
- ◆ Discussion and research into why various characters wear various clothes.
- ◆ Uses of clothing—protective, decorative.
- ◆ Assigning a value to each letter of the alphabet and calculating the value of each character's name.
- ◆ Write a story about two of these characters meeting.
- ◆ Care of your feet.
- ◆ Printing with your feet.

5

◆ MODELLENE MARKERS ◆

Year Level:	Years 3 to 6
Minimum Number of Lessons:	4
Art Concepts/Skills:	◆ Changing shape in three dimensions ◆ Decoration with shape, colour and pattern
Maths Concepts/Skills:	◆ Review of number facts ◆ Measurement in centimetres

◆ LESSON 1 ◆

Concepts/Skills	◆ Changing shape in three dimensions
Equipment	Modellene (Fimo is an alternative) (see *Special Comment*), sheet of scrap paper per child to protect the table from stains (computer paper sliced with a trimmer is ideal), scissors, 'Changing Sausages' chart, plastic lids no bigger than a milk bottle cap.
Special Comment	Modellene is a colourful modelling dough which will probably be available in your art room. If not, it can be found at the local craft shop. Small amounts of this

material go a long way provided the children are taught to use it correctly, and this is the purpose of the first lesson.

Activity

1 The first thing to learn is that Modellene uses the heat from the modeller's hands to become pliable. (Children should have clean hands when they begin.) If the Modellene is new or hasn't been used for some time, it can be quite crumbly. This is easily cured by placing a small amount (about a teaspoonful) in between the hands and rubbing the hands together. The crumbly pieces will soon join together and soften.

2 For the following activities, issue children with approximately a desertspoon of Modellene. Explain that they each have only one colour while they are getting used to using it. The Modellene will all be recovered at the end of the lesson.

In the next lesson issue a range of colours so that the children can make something permanent.

Throughout these activities, encourage fine and delicate work.

3 Demonstrate how to make a sausage of Modellene. Use a very small amount (half a teaspoon), soften it as explained, then place it on the paper which is protecting the table. Using the index finger of each hand, roll it backwards and forwards while gently moving your fingers apart to stretch the dough. The Modellene stretches a remarkable distance without breaking, as long as you keep your fingers working on the thicker areas. This amount should make a sausage which stretches right across the computer paper.

Ask the children to make three or four of these sausages.

4 Show the children a chart like the one opposite.

Encourage them to experiment with changing their sausages.

5 Show the children how to flatten out Modellene by working it between their thumb and index finger to make a pancake.

Ask them to make four pancakes about 2 mm thick.

6 Encourage the children to change their pancakes as follows:

◆ roll one to make an ice-cream cone shape. Curve the wider end decoratively;

◆ fold the sides up to make a bowl;

◆ fringe one with scissors and bend it into an interesting sculpture;

◆ use a lid to cut a circle from one. The dough will have to be prised from the lid with the scissors in the same manner as a cake is prised from its tin after baking. Cut a 'pie slice' from the circle and fold and join it to make a witch's hat. Change the 'pie slice' and use it to decorate the hat.

7 When recovering the Modellene, cardboard egg cartons make good receptacles if the children first work their colour into a ball.

◆ LESSON 2 ◆

Concepts/Skills
◆ Changing shape in three dimensions
◆ Decoration with shape, colour and pattern

Equipment
Modellene in egg cartons with the colours separated—one carton between four to six children, paper to protect tables, scissors, small plastic lids.

Activity
1 Be sure the children's hands are clean. Tell them to clean their hands again each time they finish with a dark colour so that the dye doesn't transfer to a light colour and spoil it.

2 Explain to the children that they are going to make their own marker to use in mathematical games—the sort of thing you use to move around a Monopoly board. It can be a person, a cartoon character, a creature or a transport model. It must

These markers were made by Shona, Year 3

stand on a base no bigger than a milk bottle cap and it can be no taller than their little finger. Encourage them to use plenty of detail and remind them that the colours join by being touched together and don't have to be pressed several times. If the children have trouble making their markers stand up, suggest they lean it against something, or sit it on something, or kneel it down.

3 As the children finish, they place their model on an oven tray covered with aluminium foil. Models are cooked in an ordinary oven at 325°F (160°C) for 10 minutes per half inch (1.5 cm) thickness. *Note:* Watch carefully. Rising smoke indicates overcooking. Models must not touch each other. Remove from the oven when ready and allow to cool. Models should be quite solid, although they will break if pieces are pulled at roughly.

◆ LESSON 3 or 4 ◆

Concepts/Skills
◆ Decoration with colour and pattern
◆ Review of number facts
◆ Measurement in centimetres

Equipment
Card suitable as a base for a board game, precut rectangles for writing number fact questions, rulers, pencils, Modellene markers, dice, reproducible game board (see p. 42).

Activity
1 Show the children the 'Pirate Chest' trail game. Explain that first they have to make the cards which are mentioned in the game. Issue rectangles and explain the questions that you want on the cards. Anything relevant to the group's current mathematics learning is fine.

PIRATE CHEST

START

Set sail for the treasure Jump 2 spaces

You catch lots of fish for the crew. Have another turn.

Take a card

You land on the wrong island Go back 3 spaces

Take a card

Take a card

Take a card

Take a card

Take a card

Take a card

You are hit by a terrible storm Crash on rocks Go back 5 spaces

Pirate ship! You must hide and miss a turn

Take a card

Take a card

Take a card

You land on the pirate island Have another turn

Take a card

A strong wind Go – forward 4 spaces

2 Allow the children to play the game. Some suitable rules are:

- ◆ roll a six to start
- ◆ remain on 'take a card' until you answer a question correctly
- ◆ if you land on the same square as another player, send them back to the start
- ◆ you must land exactly on the Pirate Chest to win.

The children may wish to agree on other rules.

3 Discuss with the children other topics which would be good for a trail game, as well as alternative trail designs.

Is it necessary for all the spaces in the trail to be next to each other like they are in 'Pirate Chest'?

4 Ask the children to design their own trail game as carefully as they can.

Throughout the year the games can be used many times for different purposes simply by making new packs of cards. The children are motivated by using their own game and their own marker.

Games can be made even more permanent by laminating them at a local school support centre.

◆ EXTENSIONS ◆

- ◆ Each time a card pack is made, make the corresponding answer pack too. The combined packs can then be used for Snap or Concentration.

- ◆ Children can make Personal Spelling Packs and use these when they play their games.

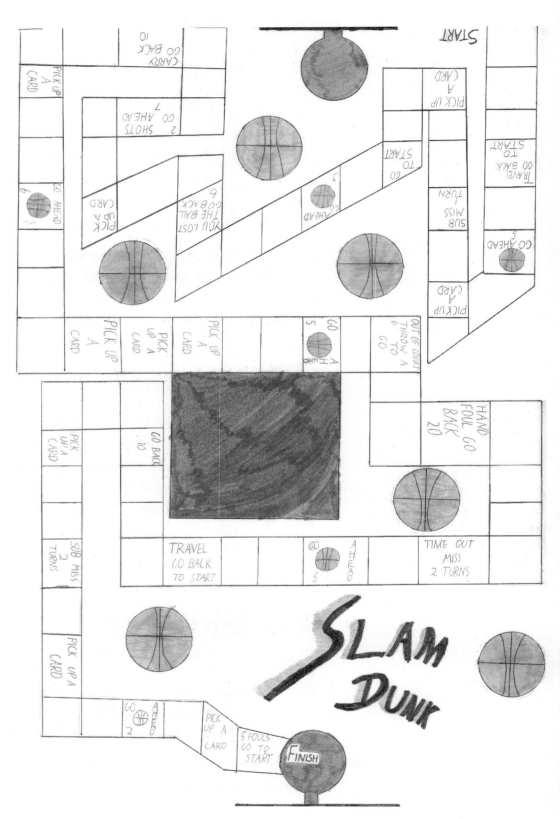

Slam Dunk.
Ian, Dean and Simon,
Year 3

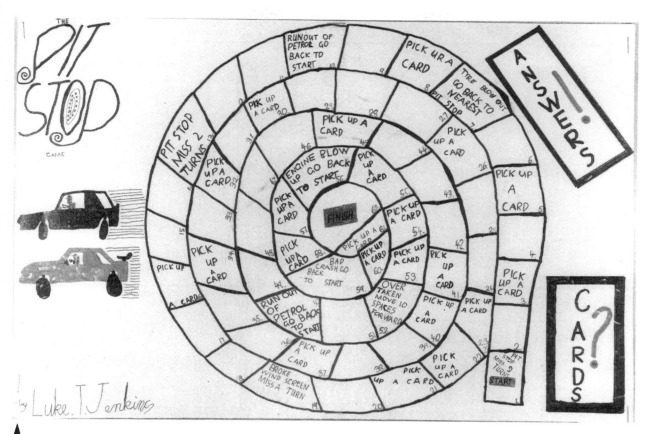

Pitstop.
Luke, Year 3

Question and Answer cards from Pitstop
▼

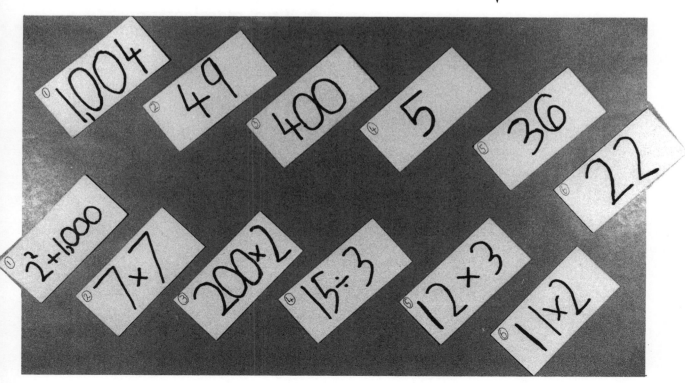

6

◆ KNOT A PROBLEM ◆

Year Level:	Year 3 or 4
Minimum Number of Lessons:	8
Art Concepts/Skills:	◆ Changing lines ◆ Contrasting lines ◆ Decoration with lines
Maths Concepts/Skills:	◆ Length measurement using formal units smaller and larger than one metre ◆ Visual representation

◆ LESSON 1 ◆

Concepts/Skills ◆ Changing lines

Equipment Balls of wool and/or string.

Activity Teach the children to finger knit. Many will already know how and can help others. This is not a difficult skill to learn and the children find it self-motivating.

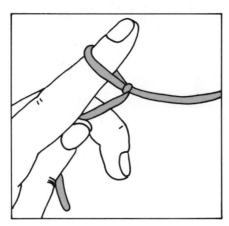

First, tie a loop of one end of your wool around your index finger and make a secure knot.

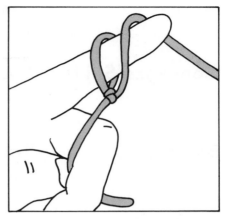

Then lift the longer part of your wool over your finger in front of this loop. Do not make a knot this time.

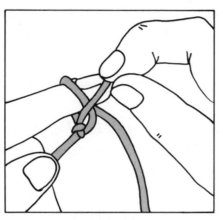

Lift the first, back loop up and forward over the front loop and drop it off your finger.

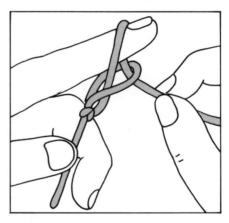

This makes your first knitted stitch. Pull your bottom short thread gently down to tighten the stitch.

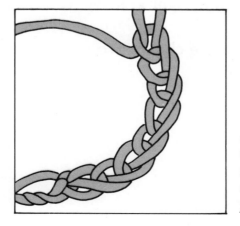

Lift more wool over in front of the loop you have left on your finger and lift the back loop over and off again. Repeat this until you have a long chain.

*From *Fun With Wool* published by the Australian Wool Corporation

◆ LESSON 2 ◆

Concepts/Skills
- ◆ Changing lines
- ◆ Length measurement smaller than one metre

Equipment

Two or more metre-rulers attached end to end to a bench or ledge, wool.

Activity

1 *Cut a piece of wool as long as your arm. Guess how long it is and write down your guess. Then measure it on the classroom ruler and write down the measurement.*

   The teacher should observe and, if necessary, correct the children's measuring techniques.

2 *Finger knit your piece of wool.*

3 *Guess the length of the finger-knitted piece of wool. Record your guess and then measure it to check your guess.*

4 Discuss the class results. Did finger knitting change the length of the wool? Did everyone's wool shorten? Did everyone's wool shorten by the same amount? Can the differences be explained? (Loose/tight knitting, wool thickness.)

5 Ask the children to write a report on the activity.

◆ LESSON 3 ◆

Concepts/Skills
◆ Changing lines
◆ Length measurement smaller than one metre
◆ Visual representation

Equipment
Wool, graph axes prepared on the chalkboard.

Activity

1 *The length of finger knitting for today is 41 cm (or some other length). Start knitting now and stop when you think your knitting has reached that length.*

2 *Measure and record the amount you actually knitted.*

3 The teacher collects and graphs data from the class. It might take this form:

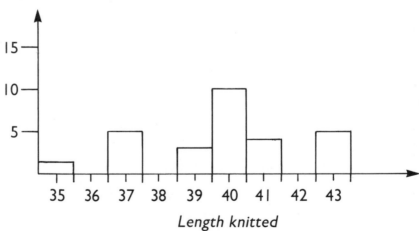

Number of people

Length knitted

4 Ask the children to write a report on the activity. If you want them to include the graph, then axes prepared and copied by the teacher is a good idea. (See reproducible sheet on p. 50.)

5 Keep the graph on the board, and keep the finger knitting for the next lesson.

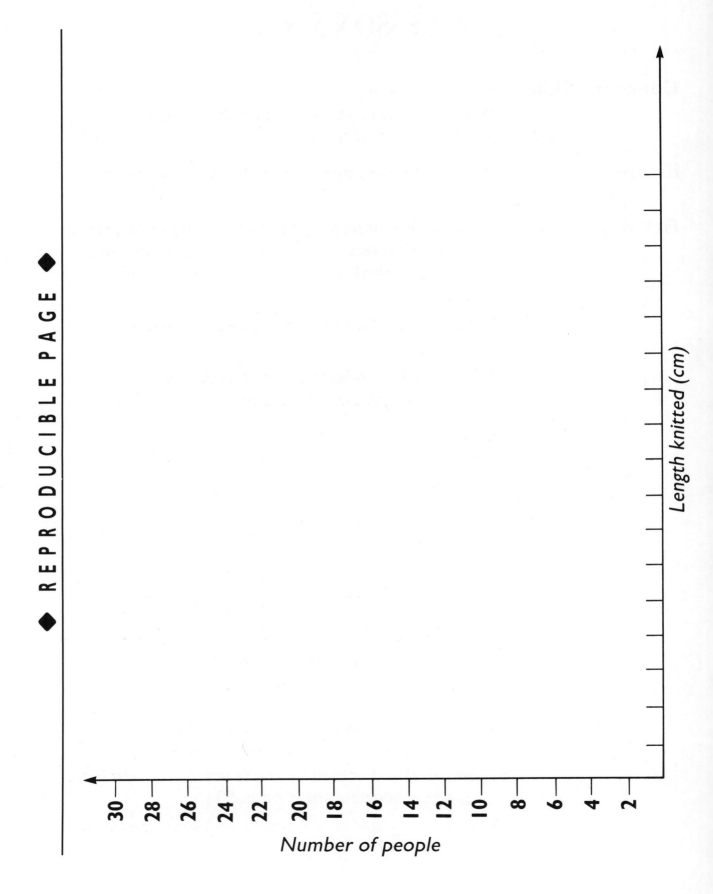

Length knitted (cm)

Number of people

30
28
26
24
22
20
18
16
14
12
10
8
6
4
2

◆ LESSON 4 ◆

Concepts/Skills
◆ Length measurement larger than one metre
◆ Visual representation

Equipment
Individual finger knitting from previous lesson, graph from previous lesson.

Activity

1 *Suppose we put all the finger knitting from the last lesson end to end, how could we find out the total length?*

Allow the children to discuss this problem in groups and then contribute approaches to a class discussion.
◆ Some may suggest laying it out and measuring with a long tape;
◆ Some may suggest adding everyone's measurement on a calculator;
◆ Some may suggest using a combination of multiplication and addition of the information in the graph prepared in the last lesson.

2 Teachers may wish to let various groups try various methods or they may prefer the class to agree on a single method. But whichever method is used, each child should guess the total first, and these guesses should be recorded.

3 The guesses could be recorded against each child's name on a line graph. (The reproducible sheet on p. 52 provides one such format.)

Before recording, the children could be asked to arrange themselves in order from smallest guess to largest and then the line graph will show a corresponding increase. The actual measurement could be added in a different colour later for comparison.

4 *Tonight I want you to finger knit for your homework. Do as much as you can. Perhaps your knitting will be as long as the netball court.*

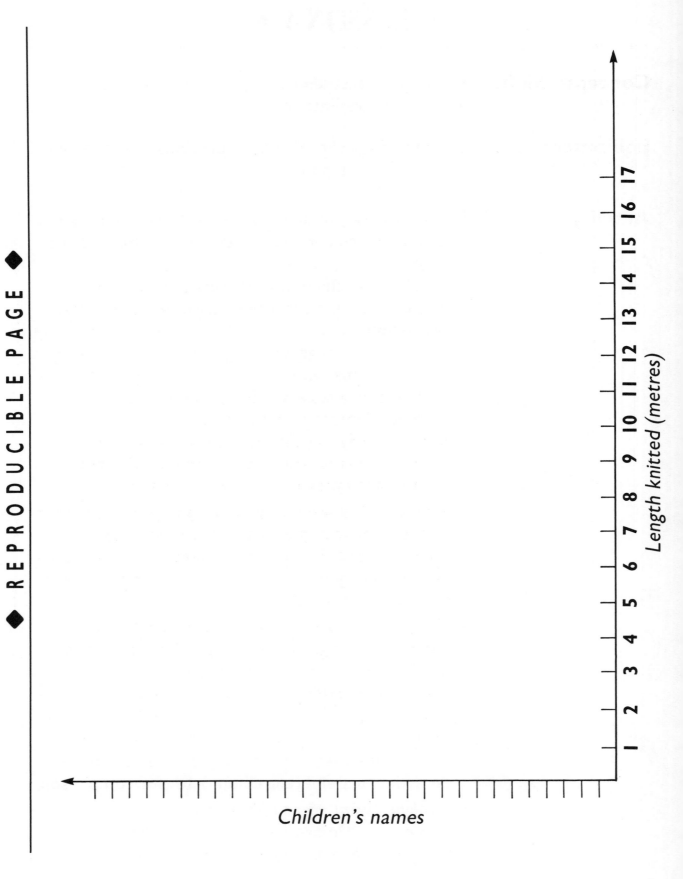

Children's names

Length knitted (metres)

◆ LESSON 5 ◆

Concepts/Skills
◆ Visual representation
◆ Length-measurement larger than one metre

Equipment
Finger knitting done at home, name card for each child, outdoor area with a suitable base line, jotter pads, trundle wheels, long tapes.

Activity

1 Ask the children to lay out their strings of knitting on the outdoor area so that they all start at the same base line. Each child places their name card on the base line next to their string.

2 *What mathematical questions could we ask another class about this graph?*
    Make a list.

3 Ask the children to rearrange their strings so the graph shows an ascending order.
    Can you think of any other questions now?

4 If possible, arrange with another class to come out and answer the children's questions. Each member of your class could pair up with a member of the other class to answer one question. If another class cannot be organised, then ask the children to answer their own questions.
    Note: Some discussion about the need to mark out a 'ruler' along the edge of the outside area would be a good start to this activity.

◆ LESSON 6 ◆

Concepts/Skills
- ◆ Changing lines
- ◆ Visual representation
- ◆ Length measurement smaller than one metre

Equipment
Strips of card about 5 cm x 50 cm, wool, rulers, pencils and pens, staplers.

Activity

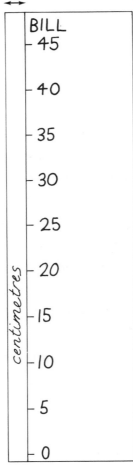

one ruler width

1 Ask each child to mark out a cardboard strip as a ruler in 5 cm jumps and write their name at the top.

2 *Today we are going to have a finger knitting race. Tie the wool to your finger, but don't start yet. You are going to knit for five minutes and I'll time you. We'll listen to some music while we race and I'll race too. Ready ... set ... GO!*

3 After the five minutes, each child ties off their knitting and staples it onto their own ruler, starting at zero. The children can also write their actual length knitted under their name.

4 Display the rulers with their knitting attached to make a bar graph.

5 Ask each child to prepare a worksheet of questions about the bar graph. These should be suitably decorated.

6 The children swap their worksheets with a friend and complete a worksheet each.

◆ LESSON 7 ◆

Concepts/Skills
- ◆ Length measurement smaller and larger than one metre
- ◆ Length measurement applied to perimeter

Equipment

Finger knitting lengths from previous lessons, boxes, cans and other objects.

Activity

1 Discuss the perimeter concept. Demonstrate how to measure the perimeter of an object with a length of finger knitting, and then take it to the classroom ruler to read off the actual measurement.

2 Children guess and measure the perimeter of four or five objects and write a report.

3 Choose a large object in the schoolyard, such as a portable classroom, and discuss the problem of finding its perimeter with the longer pieces of finger knitting from previous lessons. Then carry out the activity.

◆ LESSON 8 ◆

Concepts/Skills
- ◆ Contrasting lines
- ◆ Decoration with lines

Equipment

All the leftover finger knitting from previous lessons, Bulky News paper about 28 cm x 38 cm, wallpaper paste in containers, newspaper or plastic to protect the floor, markers, scissors.

Activity

1 Discuss with the children the lines they can make with a piece of finger knitting. As the children make some, sketch them on the board.

2 Teach the children how to shorten finger knitting by tying two thumb knots near each other and cutting in between.

3 Ask the children to create an abstract picture which shows interesting lines of finger knitting. The lengths are dipped in wallpaper paste and tapped onto the paper in the desired shape.

4 When these are dry (which can take several days), additional patterns can be added with markers.

5 Alternatively, the children could make pictures like the one shown opposite.

Elysia, Year 1 and Olivia, Year 4, with some adult help

◆ EXTENSIONS ◆

- ◆ Weaving 'God's Eyes'.
- ◆ Uses of lines in our world, e.g. tram lines, power lines, lining up.
- ◆ The five lines of the musical stave.
- ◆ Branching lines, e.g. trees, railways, family trees.
- ◆ Straight lines which make curves, e.g.

- ◆ Curve stitching.

7

◆ TWISTS AND TURNS ◆

Year Level:	Year 3 or 4
Minimum Number of Lessons:	8
Art Concepts/Skills:	◆ Decoration with line, colour and shape ◆ Contrasting lines and shapes
Maths Concepts/Skills:	◆ Exploring reflection (symmetry) ◆ Exploring rotation (pattern) ◆ Measurement in centimetres ◆ Number facts

◆ LESSON 1 ◆

Concepts/Skills
- ◆ Decoration with colour and shape
- ◆ Exploring reflection

Equipment
Paper about 28 cm x 38 cm, paint in at least three colours (fluorescent paint works well), spoons, scissors, newspapers (preferably many copies of the same paper so that print style is consistent), margarine containers (or alternative for storing), drying space.

Special Comment

Many teachers make paint blob pictures with the children but do nothing further with them. The first 3 lessons show how to turn their art into something mathematically and artistically beautiful.

Activity

1 Paint and spoons should be set up at a 'station' so that the children can file past as in a cafeteria. There should be several colours, but each child must select only two. (Three or more colours tend to blend into a dull brown or grey.)

2 The children carefully fold their paper in half and then unfold it. They are invited to splodge, drip and drag two big spoonfuls of paint onto their paper, return to their seat, fold again, press and unfold.
   These blob pictures are then left to dry.

3 Discuss with the children what they noticed about their blob pictures. Emphasise 'balance', 'same on both sides', 'like a mirror'.
   Introduce the word symmetric for shapes or patterns which have, or could have, a fold line down or across the middle.

4 Hold up a newspaper with a clear headline. *Who can tell me the symmetric letters in this headline? Which ones are not symmetrical?*
   Make lists. Classify the letters into horizontal and vertical symmetry. (It may be necessary to have some precut letters so that the children who are unsure of the idea can be given letters to fold and test the symmetry or non-symmetry.)

5 Show the children how to cut roughly around the symmetric letters and then trim carefully.
   Each pair of children then cuts out as many symmetric letters as they can, separating them into containers for horizontal and vertical symmetric letters.

◆ LESSON 2 ◆

Concepts/Skills
- ◆ Decoration with line and colour
- ◆ Contrasting lines and shapes
- ◆ Exploring reflections

Equipment Pictures of tribal masks from the library, blob pictures from the previous lesson, scissors, black cover paper about 28 cm x 38 cm, clag, fine black markers (or black biros), silver/gold markers.

Activity

1 Show pictures of tribal masks and discuss their symmetry.

2 *Today we are going to make some tribal masks of our own. We will start with our blob picture. First fold your picture in half again along the same line. Note:* Thick, dry paint on the crease can make this difficult. It is important only that the other edges match. The fold **does not** have to be pressed flat.

3 The children now cut zig-zags, curves and points around the edges, but not around the fold line. Both halves of the paper are cut simultaneously.

4 *Now use your black pen to outline some of the paint blobs. Remember though that if the mask is to be symmetrical, then what you draw on one half will have to match the other.*

5 Use the silver and gold to add more symmetric patterns. Because these are spirit-based they will draw on top of the paint.

   Children should not draw eyes however, because these will feature in the next lesson. But they can imagine where the eyes will go.

6 *Fold your black paper in half carefully and then unfold it again.*

   Now paste your mask onto the black so that the fold lines match.

Paint in here. Close together and cut.

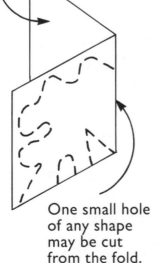

One small hole of any shape may be cut from the fold.

7 To finish this lesson children may use silver or gold on the edge of the mask where it meets the black.

◆ LESSON 3 ◆

Concepts/Skills
◆ Decoration with colour and shape
◆ Exploring reflections

Equipment
Masks from the previous lesson, symmetric letters from Lesson 1, kindergarten squares, clag, PVA glue, staplers, wool, ribbon, feathers, lids, and any other colourful material you can obtain.

Activity

1 *In many of the tribal masks we looked at, the eyes were very important. We are going to make our mask have important eyes by standing them up from the paper. Look at all this equipment I have here. Who could think of a way to make eyes stand up?*

Discuss gluing on lids, making paper cones or 'plaiting' paper to make jack-in-the-box springs. The children will suggest other methods too.

2 The children make eyes for their mask.
Remind them again to aim for symmetry.

3 The children attach symmetrically any other colourful material they wish to complete the mask.

4 Finally children hunt through their collection of vertically symmetric letters to make a vertically symmetric name for their mask.
Some possibilities are:
MUM   TOOT   VOHOV
The letters are glued to a colourful piece of paper and stapled to the bottom centre of the mask.

5 Display the results.

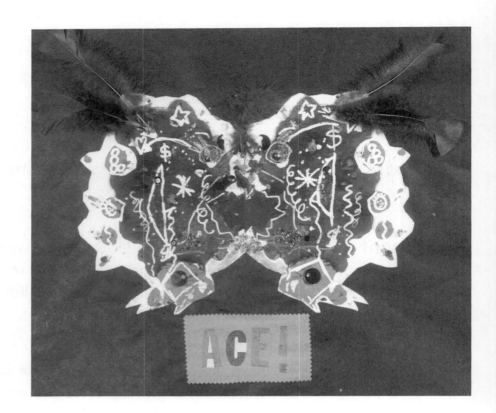

**ACE by Shona
Year 3**

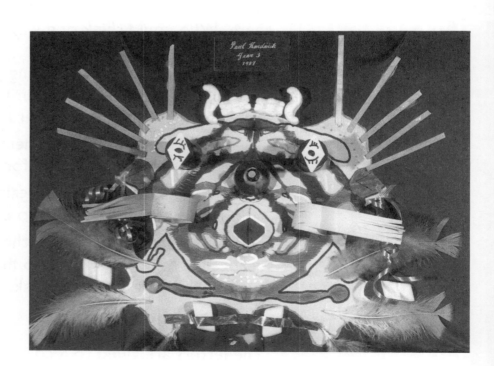

**Untitled by Paul
Year 3**

◆ LESSONS 4 and 5 ◆

Concepts/Skills
◆ Exploring symmetry
◆ Contrasting lines and shapes

Equipment
White drawing-paper about 28 cm x 38 cm, HB pencils, erasers, fine black biro or marker, copies of Picasso paintings showing asymmetric faces and bodies.

Special Comment
Frequently, in our desire to teach a particular concept, we forget to explore the counter example. Yet in many cases consideration of the counter example helps to enrich the children's understanding of the concept we are trying to teach.

In these lessons asymmetry will be explored mathematically and artistically.

Activity

1 *The faces we have made are symmetrical. Are our own faces symmetrical? Find a partner and check.*
   Discuss the children's comments. You may have to agree that human faces are **mostly** symmetrical.

2 *Soon you are going to draw your partner's face, but let's look at faces in a little more detail first.*
   Using various children as examples, discuss and record:
   ◆ various face, eye, mouth and nose shapes
   ◆ relative positions of facial features, e.g. eyes level with top of ears
   ◆ other features such as creases, hair, glasses, hair ribbons.
   The teacher may like to build up a sketch during the discussion.

3 The children now work in pairs, sitting opposite to draw each other's faces in the following way:
- ◆ fold the paper in half lengthwise to represent the facial line of symmetry
- ◆ draw one side of your partner's face with a pencil while they are modelling
- ◆ when both have finished, open out the paper and complete the face using what is known about symmetry
- ◆ when happy with the pencil drawing, trace over it with biro or marker and carefully erase any excess pencil marks.

Note: Teachers may like to break the lesson here.

Year 3 faces

Emma by Jackie

Jackie by Emma

Ian by Dean

Dean by Ian

4 To demonstrate asymmetry, ask the children to refold their work and make one face made up of half from each person.
  Is your new face symmetrical?

5 Allow the children to mix and match their half faces with other children in the class.
  If you find a new face you really like, you can give me the two halves and I will photocopy them for you.
  These would make a very interesting display!

6 *Do you think this sort of asymmetric face would be used in art?*
  Discuss the children's responses and introduce them to the work of Picasso.

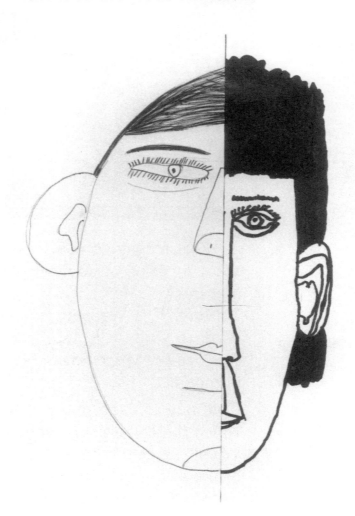

Tim plus Kevin, Year 3

Pablo Picasso (1881–1973)
Spanish, *Weeping Woman*,
1937, oil on canvas,
55 x 46 cm.
Purchased through the Art
Foundation of Victoria, with
the generous assistance of
the Jack & Genia Liberman
Family, & Donors to the Art
Foundation of Victoria, 1986.
National Gallery of Victoria,
Melbourne. © DACS 1990

What feeling do you think Picasso was trying to show by using these faces with contrasting features?

Note: 'The Weeping Woman' could be a useful work to study. It is important to realise that this was painted when Spain, Picasso's home, was being bombed.

7 Continue to explore the shapes, lines and patterns which the children can find in Picasso's work. When the children come to understand something of the background to a particular work, they may be asked to write stories or poems which the character in the painting might have written.

◆ LESSON 6 ◆

Concepts/Skills
- ◆ Exploring rotations
- ◆ Measurement
- ◆ Decoration with line

Equipment   9 cm square cards (six per child), rulers, markers.

Activity

1 Ask the children to put dots on each edge of the cards so that every edge is divided into three equal parts. (The dots will of course be 3 cm apart.)

2 Now on one card join all the dots with straight or curved lines to make a tile design, e.g.

 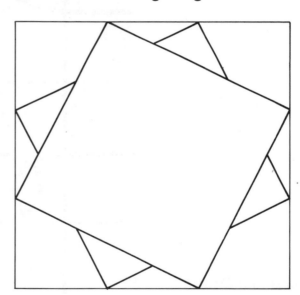

Remember all dots must be used.

3 The children now repeat their design on the five other cards.

4 Allow the children to play with their six tiles to make two rows of three.
   By changing the orientation of their tiles they can create many patterns.

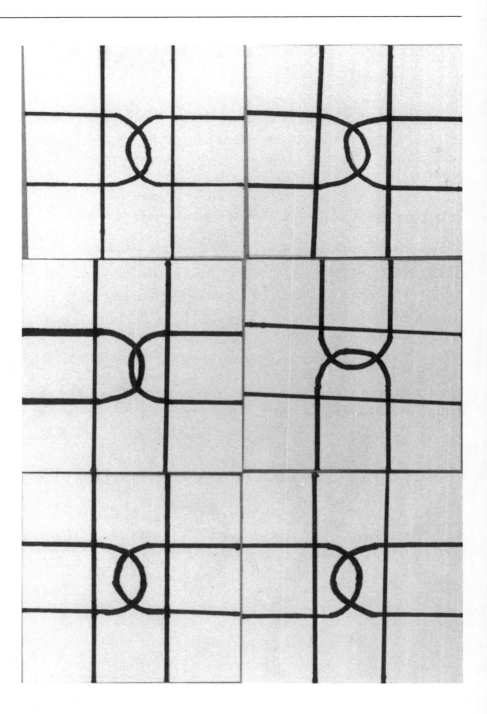

*Robert and Daniel,
Year 3*

5 *Now put your tiles in a line so that they all look
the same. Put a tiny pencil dot in the bottom left
hand corner of each tile.*

6 *Now change your tiles by making some rules about
the position of the dot.*

Robert, Year 3

For example:

	BL	BR	BL	BR	BL	BR
or	BL	TL	TR	BR	BL	TL
or	BL	TR	BL	TR	BL	TR

7 Try putting the tiles into a 2 x 3 array and changing them by making rules about the dot.

*Tile designs made by
Year 3 children*

◆ LESSON 7 ◆

Concepts/Skills
- ◆ Exploring rotations
- ◆ Number facts
- ◆ Contrasting lines

Equipment
Line design cards from the last lesson, jotter pads, pens, calculators.

Activity

1   Two children swap three cards each. Each child then has three of their own and three of a partner's. They each now explore the new designs they can make.

2   Three children swap two cards each and explore the new designs they can make. After suitable exploration time the children return the cards to their owners and stay as a group of three for the next activity.

3   Each member of the group contributes three cards to a 3 x 3 array. The members arrange the cards to make a pleasing design.

   The aim of this game is to have six of your cards in the design. The rules are:

(a)   If it is your turn you can ask either of the other players any maths question you like. It may be written down.

(b)   If they **can't** answer it (calculators can only be used for checking), you take one of their cards out of the array, give it back to them and put in one of yours.

(c)   If they **can** answer it, they take one of your cards out of the array, give it back to you and put in theirs.

(d)   If the person you ask can't answer your question, they can **challenge** you to answer it. If you answer correctly, you may remove **two of their cards**, but if you don't they may remove **two of yours**.

(e)   Players may agree on a time limit for answering questions.

Nicole, Year 3

Ian, Year 3

◆ LESSON 8 ◆

Concepts/Skills   ◆ Contrasting lines

Equipment   Cover paper about 38 cm x 56 cm and 38 cm x 28 cm, blank 9 cm square cards, line design cards from the last lesson, rulers, pencils.

Activity

1 First ask the children to make three more tiles showing their design.

2 Ask the children to explore all the pictures they can make with their tiles letting just one piece look out of place. These may be in any configuration — ordered, scattered horizontal, vertical, oblique, array, array with a missing piece.

3 Finally the children choose their favourite out-of-place arrangement and glue it to an appropriate piece of cover paper.

4 Display the out-of-place art.

◆ EXTENSIONS ◆

◆ Use the horizontally symmetric letters to make horizontally symmetric words.

◆ Play the 3 x 3 line design grid game with spelling words.

◆ Ask pairs of children to create a mirror dance.

◆ Discuss the rotation of the earth.

◆ Adapt this work to a unit on **turning**
  - turning corners
  - turning over a new leaf
  - turning up
  - turning your back on trouble etc.

8

◆ CIRCULATION ◆

<table>
<tr><td>Year Level:</td><td>Year 5 or 6</td></tr>
<tr><td>Minimum Number of Lessons:</td><td>5</td></tr>
<tr><td>Art Concepts/Skills:</td><td>◆ Changing circles
◆ Decoration with line, shape, colour and pattern
◆ Contrasting shape and colour</td></tr>
<tr><td>Maths Concepts/Skills:</td><td>◆ Number facts
◆ Visual representation
◆ Mathematics of the circle
◆ Problem-solving</td></tr>
</table>

◆ LESSON 1 ◆

Concepts/Skills
◆ Number facts
◆ Problem-solving

Equipment
The reproducible 0-9 Guzinta Clocks sheet (see p. 75), fine markers or coloured pencils, rulers.

Activity
1 Beside the first clock write the products (answers) of the 1-times table, i.e. 0 1 2 3 4 5 6 7 8 9 10.

Guzinta Clocks

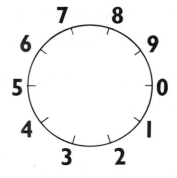
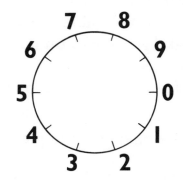
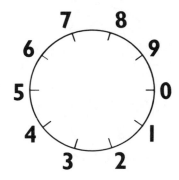

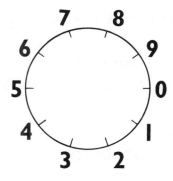
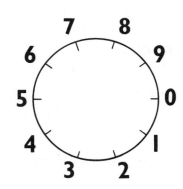
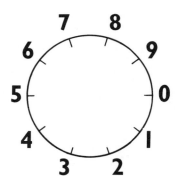

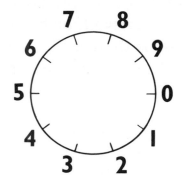
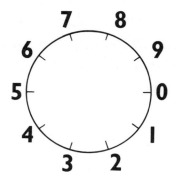
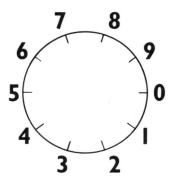

*To be enlarged on photocopier before distribution.

Beside the second clock write the products of the 2-times table, i.e. 0 2 4 6 8 10 12 14 16 18 20.

Continue this process to the ninth clock.

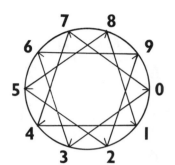

2 Now for each clock begin with zero and rule a line from this point to the final digit of the next number in the times table. Then from this one to the next final digit and so on until the pattern takes you back to zero.

Thus the 3-times table would be joined like this:

0-3-6-9-2-5-8-1-4-7-0

and would give the picture as shown.

3 Discuss with the children which drawings are simplest and which are more complex.

Write a list on the board of the agreed order from simplest drawing to most complex.

What would the 10-times table look like on one of these clocks?

Where would that picture fit in our list?

How does this list compare with the times tables you find easy or difficult to remember?

4 *Have you noticed anything else about these pictures?*

The children will readily see that certain times-tables pictures are the same.

The 2-times table and the 8-times table pictures (for example) look the same, but have they been made in exactly the same way? Is there a connection between 2, 8 an the number of points on the circle?

5 *If there is a connection in the pictures, then perhaps there is a connection in the actual times tables. See if you can find one. Work with a partner if you like.*

Allow the children to investigate for themselves for some time. If nothing fruitful develops you might suggest writing the two tables out like this:

	2×	8×
0	0	0
1	2	8
2	4	16
3	6	24
4	8	32
5	10	40
6	12	48
7	14	56
8	16	64
9	18	72
10	20	80

Eventually the children will realise that there is a connection which they will express something like: *If you add a 2-times table to the same 8-times table, you get the same 10-times table.*

or

If you take the 2-times table away from the same 10-times table, you get the 8-times table.

6 Ask the children to investigate the other complements in the times tables and write a report on their work.

◆ LESSON 2 ◆

Concepts/Skills ◆ Changing circles
◆ Contrasting shape and colour

Equipment Margarine lids, reproducible Margarine Guzinta Clocks sheet (see p. 79), Artline 70 black pens (or alternative permanent black pen), scissors, black cover paper (56 cm x 38 cm is a good size), PVA glue, clag, white paper (cartridge is good), rulers.

Activity

1 Each child needs nine margarine lids from which they carefully cut the rim to leave a circular disc.

2 Each disc is placed **print side up** on the appropriate clock of the reproducible sheet on p. 79, and the child uses the Artline 70 pen to plot each times-table picture in turn onto the margarine lid as in Lesson 1.

3 Each shape is then cut from the disc. Each child will have four polygons, four stars and two half circles (from the 5-times table) which are white (or yellow).

4 Working in threes around a large sheet of black cover paper, the children make kaleidoscope patterns by sharing their shapes.

   Perhaps some interesting ones can be photographed.

5 Individually, with a smaller piece of black and their own shapes, each child makes a picture or pattern. White paper may also be cut up and added, and black marks (not colouring-in) may be added with the Artline 70 pen.

   When the children are satisfied with their picture, the pieces may be stuck down.

Margarine Guzinta Clocks

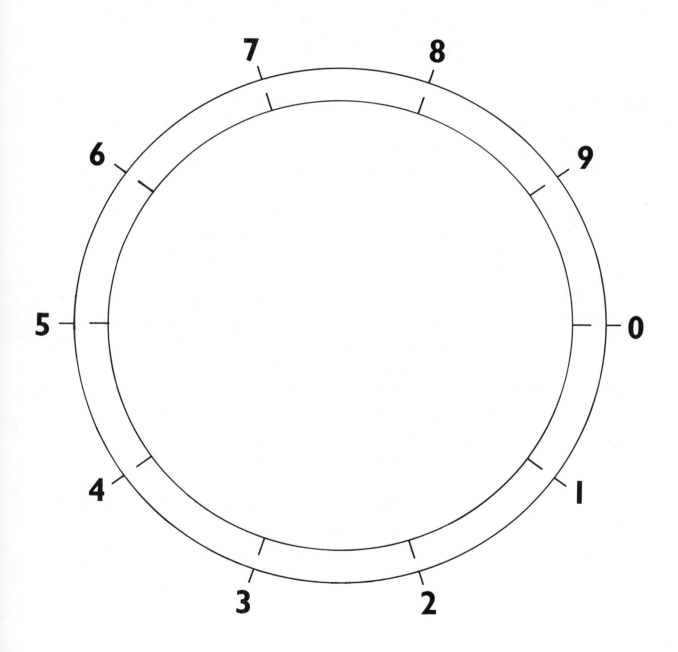

◆ LESSON 3 ◆

Concepts/Skills
- ◆ Mathematics of the circle
- ◆ Problem-solving

Equipment

An assortment of different size circles, string, metre-rulers, calculators, kindergarten squares (25 cm x 25 cm) or alternative.

Activity

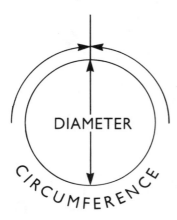

1 For each object, wrap string around the circle to measure the circumference and place it on a metre ruler to measure the diameter.
   Record the results on a chart.

2 When you have about ten results, use your calculator to find **C ÷ D** for each one.
   The result should be interesting.

3 For this part of the lesson each child needs five different size circles and three kindergarten squares. Three circles are stacked from largest to smallest on one square.
   The objective is to move the stack to one of the other squares according to these rules:

   - ◆ move one circle at a time
   - ◆ never put a big circle on top of a smaller one.

4 Children who succeed with this puzzle could try the puzzle again with five or more circles.
   (In the case of 'n' circles, the minimum number of moves is $2^n - 1$.)

◆ LESSON 4 ◆

Concepts/Skills
◆ Number facts
◆ Visual representation

Equipment
Reproducible sheet of Mixed Guzinta Clocks (see p. 82), fine markers or coloured pencils, rulers.

Activity

1 *Let's look again at one of the times-tables patterns from the first lesson. We'll choose the 7-times table.*
   Write it out on the board.
   Now how many points were there on the Guzinta Clock?
   Let's see what happens when we divide each answer in the times tables by 10 and write the remainder.

		Remainder
0	÷10	0
7	÷10	7
14	÷10	4
21	÷10	1
28	÷10	8
35	÷10	5
42	÷10	2
49	÷10	9
56	÷10	6
63	÷10	3
70	÷10	0

2 *How is this related to the pattern we drew before?*
   Join the remainders on the first circle of the Mixed Guzinta Clocks sheet to confirm that the picture is the same.

Mixed Guzinta Clocks

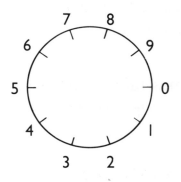 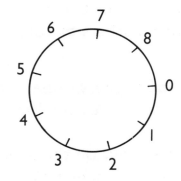 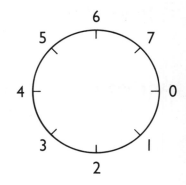

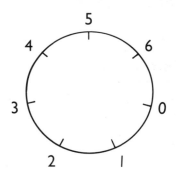 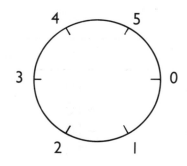 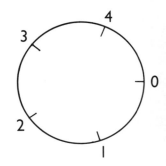

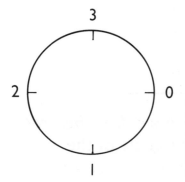 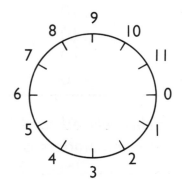 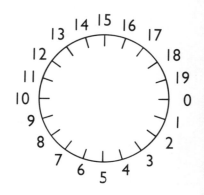

*To be enlarged on photocopier before distribution.

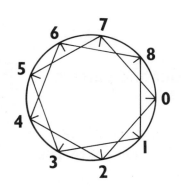

Remainders when the 7-times table is divided by 9

3 *Today you will draw the pictures for times tables divided by numbers other than 10. In each case you will draw lines which link the* **remainders** *of the divisions.*

Work through the example of the 7-times table divided by 9.

7×	Remainder after ÷9
0	0
7	7
14	5
21	3
28	1
35	8
42	6
49	4
56	2
63	0
70	7

Join the remainders on the **second circle** of the Mixed Guzinta Clocks sheet (it has nine points) to make a picture.

4 Assign each child a times table to explore. This may be done randomly or you may wish to assign particular ones to particular people because they need practice.

The clocks on the Mixed Guzinta Clocks sheet are designed for division by 10 through to 4 and division by 12 and 20. For each clock the child must rule in their workbook a chart like the one above and do a drawing on the reproducible sheet.

5 The children who have explored the same times table, meet to discuss anything they have discovered and write a brief group report.

(Save the clock sheet for the next lesson.)

◆ LESSON 5 ◆

Concepts/Skills ◆ Decoration with line, shape, colour and pattern

Equipment

Margarine lids, scissors, rulers, drawing pins, black, silver and gold permanent pens, decorative materials such as sequins, glitter and Spilloflex (thin, brightly coloured sticks which are cheaply obtainable from your school's art supplier), PVA glue, fishing line or other thread.

Activity

1 First the children must find the centre of their margarine lid. This can be done by drawing two diameters (Lesson 3) on the **printed** side and putting a pin hole where they cross.
  (The reproducible Margarine Guzinta Clocks sheet is a help.)

2 Then they cut out their most interesting drawing from Lesson 4 and find the centre of that circle.

3 Temporarily attach the centre of the drawing to the centre of the lid.

4 Use a ruler to join up the centre and each corner of the drawing, and thus place a dot for a new corner on the circumference of the **unprinted** side of the lid.

5 Remove the small drawing and join the dots in the appropriate way to make an enlargement of it on the lid in black pen.

6 This design is now decorated with the silver and gold pens or by gluing on other decorations.

7 While this is drying, each child makes another lid with the same or different design.

8 When both are dry they are glued back to back with a piece of fishing line between.
  This decoration hangs from the roof when dry.

Creating the margarine lid decoration

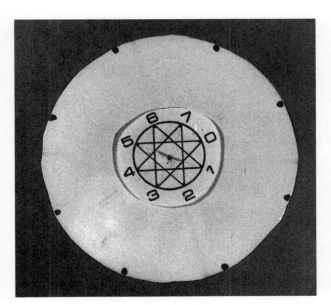

◆ EXTENSIONS ◆

- Plotting other number patterns (e.g. the squares) on Guzinta Clocks.
- Bicycle gears, ratio.
- Cycles in nature—life cycles, weather cycles, blood circulation.
- Circles as symbols—wedding rings, Olympic rings.

9

◆ SOMETHING FISHY ◆ ABOUT FRACTIONS

Year Level:	Year 5 or 6
Minimum Number of Lessons:	8
Art Concepts/Skills:	◆ Changing shape
	◆ Decoration with pattern and colour
	◆ Quality of decoration
Maths Concepts/Skills:	◆ Fraction language as part of a whole
	◆ Equivalence of fractions
	◆ Addition and subtraction of fractions

Special Comments:

◆ The mathematics lessons in this unit are based on the *Co-operative Group Learning* teaching strategy. Teachers wishing to use this approach should assign appropriate roles to group members.

Teachers not wishing to use this approach will find the lessons easy to adapt to other management techniques.

◆ I have deliberately used words rather than numerical representations of fractions throughout the unit. I believe that part of the problem we have with teaching fractions stems from using numerals too quickly—before a firm language base is constructed.

Try using written words yourself until the children agree that this method takes too long and that using numbers would be quicker.

◆ LESSON 1 ◆

Concepts/Skills
- ◆ Changing shape
- ◆ Decoration with pattern and colour
- ◆ Quality of decoration

Equipment

Large pictures of fish, pads of newspaper (when doing pastel work the drawing-paper should be rested on newspaper to obtain a better quality mark), cover paper about 28 cm x 38 cm, oil-pastels, scissors, 6B pencils (if available), sheep's wool (or some other stuffing), staplers, string.

Discussion

1 *Look at all these pictures of fish. Roughly, what shape would you say each fish is?*

Some are long, skinny ovals. Some are rounder, fatter ovals. What is added onto the oval shape?

Roughly what shape are the tail and fins?

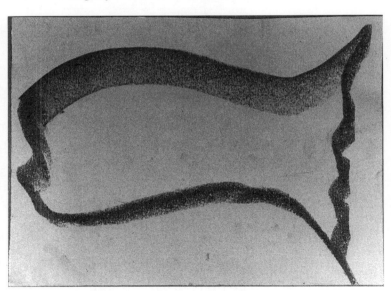

2 Fold a piece of cover paper in half and demonstrate how a fish shape can be drawn with the **side of a pastel**.

Make it as large as possible.

3 Colour the shape with the **side of the pastel** and, because every object has shades of light and dark, lighten the colour in some places and darken in others using different pastels.

4 Rub the pastel with your finger to blend the colours and remove 'paper show-throughs'. Add more pastel and rub again if necessary.
   This process creates a 'background skin' to which detail is added.

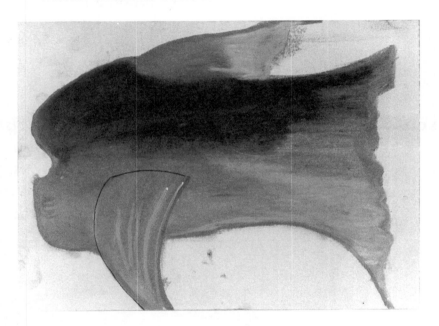

5 Study the fish pictures again and list the decoration characteristics which the children notice, e.g. eyes (circles within circles), scales, spots, stripes, bones, gills.

6 Demonstrate how these details can be added using the **end and side of the pastel**, 6B pencils (which draw on top of pastel), and/or scratch-back (scissor ends are used to scratch one layer of pastel away in a pattern to reveal another colour beneath).

Activity

1 Prepare a fish skin as discussed.

2 Decorate the skin to make the fish look as realistic as possible. Start with the eyes.

3 With the paper still folded, cut out the fish accurately.

4 Staple the two sides of the fish across the top, stuff in the off-cuts and extra sheep's wool if necessary, and staple around the rest of the fish.

5 Add a string for hanging up.

6 Make a second 'fat fish'.

7 Hang the fish from the roof in an aquarium display until they are needed in later lessons.

◆ LESSON 2 ◆

Concepts/Skills   ◆ Fraction language

Equipment   Small pieces of paper and a pen for each individual, large recording-paper and marker pens for each group.

Activity   *Note:* Teachers often become concerned about teaching fractions. It is hard to decide where to start and to determine how much children really have to know about fractions today.

This activity will quickly give you a guide to the children's current understanding of the topic and allow you to adjust your subsequent teaching. It is based on a language activity called **bundling**.

1 Give each child five small strips of paper. On each strip they write a sentence of something they know about fractions. These can vary from:
Half an apple plus half an apple is a whole apple
to
I hate fractions.
   (The children may use a picture instead of one sentence.)

2 Group the children into fours (and assign roles if using *Co-operative Group Learning*).
   The children compare their sentences and have to use about five of them to write a paragraph of important or interesting information about fractions. All the children in the group **must agree** on the inclusion of any sentence in their paragraph.
   The chosen paragraph is written out for display.

3 Display the paragraphs from each group and discuss. One point of discussion may be:
What are the things about fractions on which we all agree?

Another may be:
*How many different examples can we think of
which show this fact?*

◆ LESSON 3 ◆

Concepts/Skills
◆ Fraction language
◆ Equivalence of fractions

Equipment
Fish from previous lesson (one each), physical
education hoops or alternative to contain 'schools' of
fish, recording-paper and markers.

Activity

1 Arrange the children in groups of four with a hoop,
their fish, a marker and recording-paper.
Explain to the children that you are going to ask
some questions and the recorder has to write the
answer with which everyone in the group agrees.
The answer should be **a sentence**.

2 The children each place one of their fish in the
hoop to make a 'school' of fish.

*How many parts make
this whole school?*

Discuss the answers from various groups as the questioning proceeds.

How many parts make this whole school?

Using fraction language, what is the name of each part?

How many fourths make the whole school?

3 The class counts forwards and backwards by fourths. Make sure that the children touch each fish as they count.

4 *Now, separate your school into two equal parts. Using fraction language, what is each part called? How many halves of the school make the whole school?*

Look at one half of the school. Could you name this part in fourths? Write a sentence with an equals sign.

5 *Separate your school into three parts. (It doesn't have to be equal parts.) Write a sentence in fraction language.*

Does this separation show thirds of the whole school? Discuss and write a sentence.

◆ LESSON 4 ◆

Concepts/Skills	◆ Fraction language ◆ Equivalence of fractions
Equipment	Two fish each, hoops, recording-paper, markers.
Activity	**1** Repeat the same style of lesson as Lesson 3, but each child now gives two fish to the school. The teacher can then devise questions about eighths, fourths and halves similar to those in the previous lesson.

How many parts make this whole school?

2 To encourage understanding of the need for the parts to be equal (in number) before naming a new fraction, questions such as these could be used: *Separate the whole into six parts. Write a sentence in fraction language. Does this separation show sixths of the whole school?*

Discuss and write a sentence.

◆ LESSON 5 ◆

Concepts/Skills
- ◆ Fraction language
- ◆ Equivalence of fractions

Equipment
Three counters for each person, a tabletop 'pond' for each group (e.g. a piece of cover paper), recording-paper, markers.

Activity	**1** *We only made two fat fish each. So today, because we need three fish each to make the school, we will use counters in place of fish. The cover paper keeps the whole school together just like the hoop did.*

The children make a school of twelve parts.

2 As for Lessons 3 and 4, the teacher devises questions which the children answer as a group. This size whole allows questions about twelfths, sixths, thirds, fourths, halves.

◆ LESSON 6 ◆

Concepts/Skills	◆ Equivalence of fractions ◆ Preliminary addition and subtraction of fractions
Equipment	Counters, cover paper 'pond', reproducible sheet with many ponds (see p. 95).
Activity	*Today we will often change the size of our school. In one question the whole school might have seven fish. In another it might have four. We don't have enough fat fish, so we will use counters in place of fish.*

To answer each question your group will have to draw a picture on the pond sheet after trying out the answer with the counters on the cover paper.

The teacher now asks questions like those overleaf and the children have to reach consensus about the picture they draw.

The drawings will serve as a form of evaluation. Remember though that each question has more than one correct answer.

◆ R E P R O D U C I B L E   P A G E ◆

*To be enlarged on photocopier before distribution.

Make a school which can be separated into

- *thirds*
- *fifths*
- *sevenths*
- *thirds and sixths*
- *halves and fourths*
- *thirds and ninths*
- *halves and thirds*
- *halves and fifths*
- *thirds and fifths*
- *fourths and sixths.*

◆ LESSON 7 ◆

Concepts/Skills   ◆ Addition and subtraction of fractions

Equipment   Hoops and fat fish, or counters and cover paper, small pieces of paper and a pen for each individual, recording-paper and markers.

Activity   This is another **bundling** activity.
1 The group makes a school of fish of a chosen size — say eight parts to the whole.
2 On each small strip, each child has to write a sentence about the whole school which uses fraction language (or symbols, if that has developed), and +, − and = signs, e.g. two fourths + one half + one fourth − two eights = whole school (or $\frac{1}{4} + \frac{1}{2} + \frac{1}{4} - \frac{1}{8} = 1$).
   Each child should do about four of these.
3 The group compares their sentences and prepares a chart of the six most interesting.
4 This activity should be repeated many times, over many days, with many different size schools of fish.

◆ LESSON 8 ◆

Concepts/Skills   ◆ Addition and subtraction of fractions

Equipment   Hoops and fat fish, or counters and cover paper, recording-paper, markers.

Activity

1 The exercise in all these activities is to work out the number of parts the whole school of fish must have. The children first use their equipment to solve the mystery and then agree on a method of writing out the solution to the addition or subtraction.

2 The following problems are examples. The teacher should design many more over a number of lessons.

- *My school has a certain number of fish. I won't tell you how many, but I will tell you that I can use it to work out what one fourth of the school plus one half of the school equals. Find out the **smallest possible** number of fish in my school.*

- *My school has a certain number of fish and I can work out three fifths minus one half. Find out the **smallest possible** number of fish in my school.*

3 Discussion of the students' attempts to write out the solution to the addition and subtraction problems involved in these puzzles should lead, over a short period, to the adoption of a standard format.

◆ EXTENSIONS ◆

- Developing a classroom fish-tank.
- Fish as a food.
- Fish-farming.
- Sea shanties and other sea music.
- Make up fish stories, e.g. 'The One That Got Away'.

10

◆ MILK CARTON ◆
MATHEMATICS

Year Level:	Year 5 or 6
Minimum Number of Lessons:	5
Art Concepts/Skills:	◆ Changing shape in 3D ◆ Decoration with line and pattern
Maths Concepts/Skills:	◆ 3D geometric language ◆ Problem-solving ◆ Pattern investigation
Special Comment:	This unit requires many 1 litre and 2 litre cardboard milk cartons. Each child requires six 1 litre cartons and one 2 litre carton. (This number could be reduced if you arrange group work.) Start collecting early, but insist that the cartons are washed and **dried**, and open at the top before they are brought to school.

◆ LESSON 1 ◆

Concepts/Skills ◆ 3D geometric language
◆ Problem-solving
◆ Changing shape in 3D

Equipment

Milk cartons (1 litre), scissors, staplers, paper-clips, prism chart.

Activity

Square prism

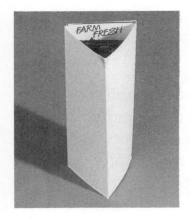

Triangular prism

Hexagonal prism

1 Ask the children to cut the pouring spout section from a carton so that it looks like the one in the picture.

   (The carton is a square prism without cutting off the pouring spout but this section has been weakened in manufacture, so it is best removed.)

   Introduce the mathematical name of this object—**square prism**—and explain why.

   Square - the shape of the base
   Prism - the sides stand at right angles to the base—like the walls of a house.

2 Show the children your prism chart and enter 'open milk carton' under the square prism heading.

   Ask the children to look for other prisms in the room, e.g. a closed book is almost a rectangular prism.

3 Ask each child to use another milk carton and, after removing the pouring section, cut right down one fold line and cut off the base.

   Then the carton is folded inside out and two flat sides are stapled on top of each other to make the shape shown.

   Ask the children what name this solid might be given.

   Add it to the chart and ask if the children know any other triangular prisms, e.g. a bar of Toblerone chocolate.

4 Group the children in sixes and ask them to use their triangular prisms to make a hexagonal prism.

   Paper-clips can be used to hold the solid together as in the photograph.

5 Ask the children to use the prisms they have made (square and triangular) and paper-clips to make new prisms, e.g. pentagonal (from one square and one triangular) or four-pointed star.

Add new ones to the chart and ask the children to bring in any prisms or other 3D objects they can find.

◆ LESSON 2 ◆

Concepts/Skills
- ◆ Pattern investigation
- ◆ 3D geometric language

Equipment

Prisms constructed during the last lesson.

Activity

1 Using the various prisms as examples, introduce the descriptive language of solid objects:
Faces - flat sides which make the walls or bases
Edges - the lines where two faces meet
Vertices - the corners.

2 *There is a rule which connects the number of faces, edges and vertices for a prism. Can you find this rule?*
Note: It is important to count the 'empty faces' which were cut away at the top and bottom.

This problem is not open-ended since there is only one expected answer (which may appear in different forms), but posing it in this way allows the teacher to observe the strategies of individuals and groups.

This could be the basis of a later class discussion.

3 Ask the children to check their rule ($F + V - E = 2$) on several objects.

Does it work on Egyptian pyramids or triangular drink boxes (like Tetra Pak or Sunny Boy)?

◆ LESSON 3 ◆

Concepts/Skills
- ◆ Decoration with shape and colour
- ◆ Changing shape in 3D

Equipment

Milk cartons from previous lessons, coloured paper, clag, PVA glue, cardboard tubes, staplers, and whatever decorative materials you can obtain.

Activity

1 This activity will change the mass of milk cartons the class has collected into objects of function and beauty.

Simply make a blackboard list of the children's suggestions about what one or more cartons could be turned into, e.g. monsters, assorted models of transport, table tidies, a Christmas tree.

The only rule is that no advertising and no sticky tape may show on the finished product.

Table tidy made by Simone, Year 5

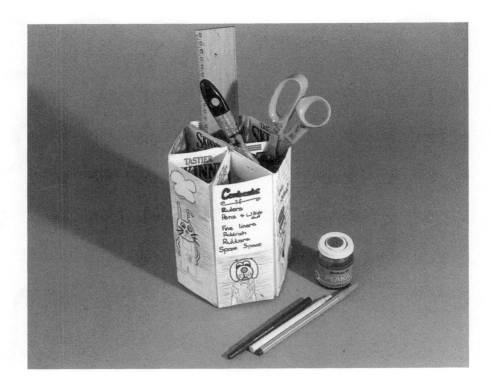

◆ LESSON 4 ◆

Concepts/Skills ◆ Decoration with line and pattern

Equipment   Milk cartons (2 litre), dead matches, fishing-line or string, rulers, scissors, staplers, hole punchers, permanent markers (silver, gold, black).

Activity

1 Make the carton into a triangular prism, as in Lesson 1, **but** before it is stapled, make a small hole in the middle of the centre fold line.

2 After it is stapled, punch a small hole in the centre of each end of the double thickness.

3 Using permanent markers, create a pattern on each face of the prism. Any of the marks shown below would be a good start, for such a pattern, and/or collections of them when repeated, make fascinating effects.

Line patterns for milk cartons

4 Some children may find it easier to draw while the carton is flat, i.e. before it is made into a prism.

5 To complete the lesson, pass a piece of fishing-line through the hole in the middle of the centre fold line and tie it to a grooved match to suspend the carton. (Groove the match by gently squeezing it with scissors.)

◆ LESSON 5 ◆

Concepts/Skills
◆ Pattern investigations
◆ Problem-solving

Equipment   Decorated cartons from Lesson 4, counters.

Activity

1 In groups of three the children join their cartons to make a mobile.

2 *This mobile has two levels. There is one carton in the first level and two in the second. How many cartons would be in the next level?*
How many in the one after that?

3 Ask the children to copy and complete the table below. Counters or some other material should be available so the children can model the situation.

Level in the Mobile	Number of Cartons at this Level
1	1
2	2
3	4
4	
5	
20	

4 When the *Number Machines* unit has been completed, children could be asked to find how the 'out number (T)' is found from the 'in number (N)'. This is quite a challenge!

5 The children could also try to complete the following table.

Level in the Mobile	Total Number of Cartons so far
1	1
2	3
3	7
4	
5	
20	

(Another challenge is to find the connection between T and N in this table!)

◆ EXTENSIONS ◆

- ◆ Build a milk carton cubbyhouse (lifesize).
- ◆ Investigate what happens when light passes through a prism.
- ◆ Packing 3D objects.
- ◆ Milk as a food.
- ◆ Constructing regular polyhedra (platonic solids).
- ◆ Writing a story based on the object made in Lesson 3.

11

◆ NUMBER MACHINES ◆

Year Level:	Year 5 or 6
Minimum Number of Lessons:	5
Art Concepts/Skills:	◆ Special effects with line ◆ Decoration with line, shape and colour
Maths Concepts/Skills:	◆ Number facts ◆ Pattern investigations ◆ Problem-solving

Special Comment:
◆ Once the number machine is created—as described in the first lessons—it can be used in many ways at many times throughout the year.

    Therefore Lessons 3 to 5 should be thought of as samples to be used as necessary, rather than as consecutive lessons.
◆ The size of the number machine may be changed to suit a small group-teaching approach.

    One way of doing this is to supply each child with a large sheet of cover paper and ask them to draw with thicker black markers such as an Artline 70 pen. (Use a sheet of newspaper under the cover paper because the marker can soak through.)

    One machine this size is big enough for four to six children to gather around.

◆ LESSON 1 ◆

Concepts/Skills ◆ Decoration with line and shape

Equipment Photographs and drawings of machines, the reproducible sample number machine sheet (see p. 109), fine black pens or ball-points, paper for sketching, glue, cartridge or cover paper about 28 cm x 38 cm, rulers, precut rectangles 5 cm x 3 cm. (Some teachers may prefer to ask the children to design their machine in pencil first. This approach will require pencils and erasers.)

Activity

1 Study together the parts of the machines in the photographs. Discuss gears, wires, levers, belts, control panels, switches, lights etc.
    Ask the children to sketch some of the shapes they see.
    How are machine shapes different from natural shapes?
    Discuss terms like regular or geometric.

2 *Today you are going to design your own machine and just like any designer, there are rules to follow.*
    First, the outside of the machine may be any shape you like, but
    (i) it must fill most of the page
    (ii) it must have only one way in and only one way out.

    Draw your machine shape now.

3 Give the children three precut rectangles each.
    Your machine is going to have many parts inside it. Here are the first three. Decorate them to look like machinery.

***Number machine
starter shapes*** ➤

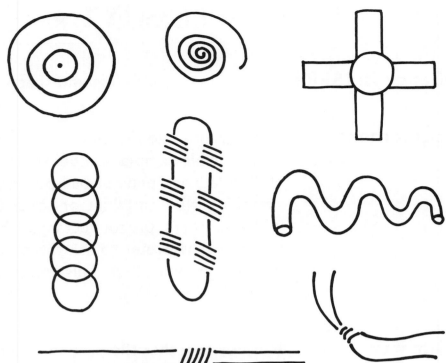

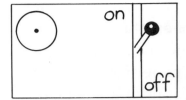

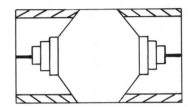

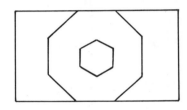

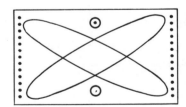

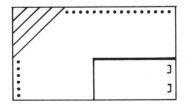

**Sample machinery
rectangles. A plastic
stencil has been used
to aid the drawing,
but this is not
essential.**

4 *Now, glue these parts inside your machine. They
may be anywhere and at any angle, but they may
not overlap.*

5 *To complete your machine design there is one final
rule: your machine must have one pathway from
IN, through the three rectangles, to OUT. Apart
from that, anything else may happen.*

*You might like to use some of the shapes you
sketched earlier or some of the ones shown above.
A finished machine might look like this.* (Distribute
copies of the sample number machine on p. 109.)

Briefly discuss the example with the children.
This works well if it has been made into an
overhead transparency.

(If the children comment on the 'sound shapes',
tell them that these will be part of the next lesson.)

Draw your machine.

A Number Machine

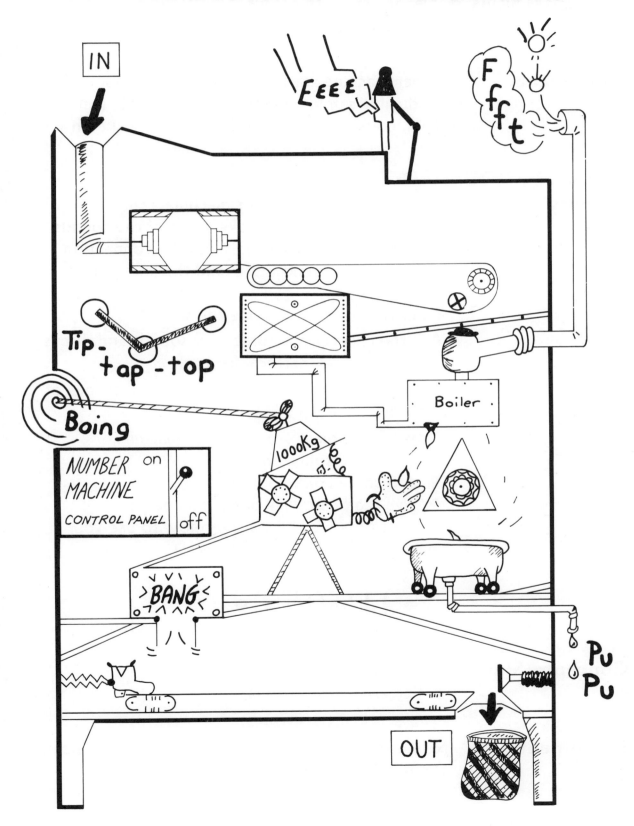

◆ LESSON 2 ◆

Concepts/Skills
- ◆ Decoration with colour
- ◆ Special effects with line

Equipment
Number machine started during the last lesson, the reproducible sample number machine sheet (see p. 109). coloured pencils and/or markers, sketch paper.

Activity

1 Show the sample number machine again.
Ask the children to make some of the sounds shown on the machine. Discuss the connection between the 'sound word' and the line pattern with it.
Does the pattern describe the sound?

2 Ask the children for some new sounds and discuss the 'sound' and 'pattern' for each.

3 Ask the children to sketch some sound shapes of their own.

4 *Now to complete your number machine,*
- ◆ *add some sound shapes*
- ◆ *add some colour*
- ◆ *give it a beautifully printed name.*
Next time we will discover how to use your machine to learn some mathematics.

◆ LESSON 3 ◆

Concepts/Skills
- ◆ Number facts
- ◆ Pattern investigations

Equipment
Number machines, precut rectangles 5 cm x 3 cm, Unifix or counters, calculators.

Activity

1 Give each child a dozen rectangles.
   Your number machine can be programmed to do mathematics by reprogramming each rectangle in your drawing with an instruction. For example, write one card which says +1 *(or* add 1 *), one which says* +2, *and one which says* +3.
   Place these on the rectangles in your drawing.

2 *Now feed 10 Unifix into the machine, follow the path, and as you come to each card, do what it commands.*
   Count the Unifix which arrive at **OUT** *and keep a record of the ins and outs, e.g.*

IN	10 . . . .
OUT	16 . . . .

3 *Feed in five more sets of Unifix, any number you want, and record the ins and outs.*

4 *Feed in zero Unifix. What comes out?*

5 *Suppose someone invented a smarter machine than yours which used one program card instead of three. What* **one card** *would have the* **same result as your three***?*
   Draw it next to your in/out chart.

6 Repeat this activity using the cards.
   −1   −2   −3.
   An additional question to ask the children is:
   What is the smallest number of Unifix you can feed in if the machine is going to work?
   Remember to ask for the one card which replaces the three.

7 Let the children carry out the activity twice more using cards which they write themselves.
   Remind them to find the one card which replaces the three each time. (Sometimes two cards must be used to replace the three.)

Note: Throughout these activities the children may sometimes have trouble finding one or two cards to replace the three.

You can

(i) suggest they feed in Unifix which make the numbers easier, or

(ii) write on the board something like:

Can anyone help Mary replace $\boxed{+2}$ $\boxed{\div 3}$ $\boxed{-4}$?

Someone will discover that $\boxed{-10}$ $\boxed{\div 3}$ works.

Once the children understand the machine, it can be used on a regular basis for a short activity simply by changing the cards.

◆ LESSON 4 ◆

Concepts/Skills	◆ Number facts ◆ Pattern investigations ◆ Problem-solving
Equipment	Number machines, precut rectangles 5 cm x 3 cm, Unifix or counters, calculators.
Activity	1 Ask the children to write a card which says $\boxed{\textbf{no change}}$ and any two others. These are placed in the machine, Unifix is fed in and a record of ins and outs is kept. *Does the* $\boxed{\textbf{no change}}$ *card affect the out number? Take it out and see if the ins and outs stay the same.* 2 *What mathematical commands can you think of which could take the place of the* $\boxed{\textbf{no change}}$ *card?* Ask the children to try an experiment with these cards $\boxed{+0}$ $\boxed{-0}$ $\boxed{\div 1}$ $\boxed{\times 1}$.

3 *Write any command card. Now write its opposite, e.g.* $\boxed{\times 3}$ *and* $\boxed{\div 3}$. *Write one extra card.*

Use all three in your machine so that it is programmed to do only what the extra card says, e.g. $\boxed{\times 3}$ $\boxed{\div 3}$ $\boxed{+20}$ *has the same effect as* $\boxed{+20}$ **but**

$\boxed{\times 3}$ $\boxed{+20}$ $\boxed{\div 3}$ **doesn't** *have the same effect as* $\boxed{+20}$.

4 With the help of a calculator, the children should investigate changing the order of their cards so that the effect is **not** the same as the extra card.

For example $\times 3$ $\;+20\;$ $\div 3$ gives this chart:

IN	1	2	3	4
OUT	7.6666666	8.6666666	9.6666666	....

So the three cards could be replaced by $\boxed{+6.6666666}$.

For interested teachers, the reason for this is straight forward. Let **N** stand for the **in number**, and **T** stand for the **out number**. Then the cards $\boxed{\times 3}$ $\boxed{+20}$ $\boxed{\div 3}$ mean multiply N by 3, then add 20, then divide all this by 3 to get T. All this can be written:

$$T = (3 \times N + 20) \div 3$$
$$= (3N \div 3) + (20 \div 3)$$
$$= N + 6\tfrac{2}{3}$$
$$= N + 6.6666666$$

since $6\tfrac{2}{3}$ on the calculator displays as 6.6666666.

5 Ask the children to think of three cards which have the same effect as $\boxed{+100}$.

Can they do it without using opposites?

Can they do it without using opposites or $\boxed{\textbf{no change}}$ equivalents?

6 Ask the children to design three cards which have the same effect as doubling N.

Can they do it without using opposites?

Can they do it without using opposites or no change equivalents?

◆ LESSON 5 ◆

Concepts/Skills
- ◆ Number facts
- ◆ Pattern investigations
- ◆ Problem-solving

Equipment
Number machines, calculators, precut rectangles 5 cm x 3 cm, worksheet (see below).

Activity
1 Write this chart on the board:

N	0	1	2	3	4	5
T	1	3	5	7	9	11

This chart has come from someone's number machine. Can you write a sentence which explains what the machine does? It might be programmed with one card, or two cards, or three cards.

Check each alternative offered to see if it works. If it does, write it out in words and then, with the help of the class, in symbols, e.g.

double, subtract 3, then add 4
becomes
$T = 2 \times N - 3 + 4$

or

double, then add 1
becomes
$T = 2 \times N + 1$

Discuss any connections which the children see.

2 Prepare a worksheet for the children to complete individually or in pairs. Questions could be of these types:

◆ *My number machine is programmed with two cards and it gives this chart. What are the cards?*

N	0	5	10	15	20
T	6	11	16	21	26

Make up examples for one and three card machines as well.

◆ *My number machine uses this rule:*

$T = 2 \times (N + 2) - 2$

Write out a chart for it.

Can you think of some other rules which work for this chart?

◆ Alternatively, discuss examples like these with the whole class, then ask each child to invent a Number Machine Puzzle for someone else to do.

Collect them, check them and publish them, with suitable acknowledgement, for the class.

Note: Although algebra appears to feature in these later lessons, they are **not meant to be algebra lessons**. The symbols are intended to flow from the children's language as a shorthand and are to be used when the children agree that they save effort and/or time.

◆ EXTENSIONS ◆

◆ Dismantling machines to find out how they work. Ask parents to supply everything from old clocks to washing machines.

◆ Discussing machines with a special purpose to make life easier, such as nappy changing machines, children waker-uppers, homework machines etc.
   The children could choose one from the discussion, draw it and then write a story based on it called 'The Day the _____ Machine Broke Down'.

◆ Build simple machines, e.g. use Technical Lego.

◆ Make lists of machine words and their companions, e.g. lever, leverage, elevator, elevate, cantilever . . . .

◆ Find out about machines invented in this country.

◆ Find out about machines which 'changed our world', e.g. the steam engine, television, computers.